T0194949

POWER DAYS

JEFFREY D. HILL

WESTBOW
PRESS®
A DIVISION OF THOMAS NELSON
& ZONDERVAN

WestBow Press books may be ordered through booksellers or by contacting:

WestBow Press
A Division of Thomas Nelson & Zondervan
1663 Liberty Drive
Bloomington, IN 47403
www.westbowpress.com
844-714-3454

ISBN: 978-1-6642-3959-3 (sc)
ISBN: 978-1-6642-3958-6 (hc)
ISBN: 978-1-6642-3957-9 (e)

Library of Congress Control Number: 2021913373

Print information available on the last page.

WestBow Press rev. date: 01/11/2022

INTRODUCTION

We all have a choice to make about how we live our lives. We decide if our lives are lived to the full, spent, wasted, invested, maximized or merely endured. By virtue of our own attitudes, we choose whether our days will be good, bad or just another day. We all have challenging days in which we have no choice but to work through them. Some days seem to fly by while others drag on making us wonder if it will ever end. There are bright, sunny days that warm us and allow us to rest while other days are cold, windy, drenched in rain or snow and days when storms rise up changing our plans altogether. One truth is common to each of those days: We must experience and live each day one at a time. The rules of life dictate that we can neither go back to relive any given day nor are we are not allowed to skip any of the days ahead. We might wish we could but jumping forward is not part of the game. We live each of our days.

Because the only choice we have is to live each day, Wisdom suggests the better choice is to do our best to ensure every day makes a real and lasting impact, not only for ourselves, but for those we connect with daily. We impact others simply by being who and what we are – ourselves. Since we're going to do that, does it not make sense that we strive to be the best version of ourselves to ensure the impact we make is a good one? I claim the easiest, best, and most effective way to be our best is to make our first connection of the day, every day, be with God, our Father.

Every morning, take in one quick note from His word. One more insight to everyday life that allows you to see your own experience from a different perspective. A snippet to remind us we're not taking this journey through life by ourselves; that we're not the only ones who had to go through *that* thing. God's word helps us to focus, to get our priorities in order, to allow our hearts to smile and strengthen our faith by His word and allow Him to cloak us in

His armor so we can take on the day from a position of power. Not our own power – God's power. Doing so ensures the day will not be just another day. It is my hope you'll be empowered and encouraged by the Word of God and the insights shared herein.

That's the purpose of this devotional. To help your day, every day, be a closer walk with God, to encourage you to begin your day with something that will help you get into His Word and give you something to ponder throughout the day. Something to strengthen you and maintain your hope. Starting your day with God helps eliminate the "just another day" syndrome and helps you walk through a day of life with energy, vigor, purpose and to make every day, a Power Day.

DEDICATION

This book is dedicated first and foremost to God for his unending grace, mercy and guiding love. To my wife, Grace, for her patience, understanding and encouragement. To my family just for being who they are and to all the people who invested their time, wisdom, advice, and love in me.

Thank you for that gift.

John 14:6, "Jesus answered, "I am the way and the truth and the life. No one comes to the Father except through me.""

If you've ever done any traveling, you know there are a wide variety of ways to travel. There are modes of transportation designed for short journeys and others specifically meant for longer journeys. Perhaps you've had the opportunity to use a few of these. In my life, I have traveled across the Atlantic Ocean numerous times by airplane and five times by ship. The first time by ship didn't go well near the end of the voyage and we had to be rescued from the wreck of the Andrea Doria, which was a whole other adventure for another day.

As youngsters, the vehicles we ride in are the arms of mom and dad or we got pushed around in a stroller. As we grew and learned to walk, we discovered all the interesting places our feet could take us. Then we got a wagon, or a Hot Wheel to ride on in the driveway. Maybe you recall Tonka trucks that kids sit on and power around with their feet. One day, we accepted the challenge of roller skates and braved all the bumps and falls we endured until we found our balance. We tried scooters, then on to skateboards, and one day, under the Christmas tree, there was that shiny new bicycle. All modes of transportation that brought us to real and imaginary places and into adventure and discovery and joy.

One magical day, we learned to drive ….a….car! YEA! Now I really am cool! I can drive! Do you remember the exhilaration of the first time you sat in the driver's seat, wrapping your hands around the steering wheel and started the engine? Like it was yesterday, right? This was independence. We could go anywhere. Maybe you were one to ride a motorcycle, too, which lead to off roading and maybe to competition. Over time, you've traveled in cars and trucks of all makes, models, sizes and colors.

How about trains? Have you traveled near or far by railway car? Ships and planes, cars and trains, bikes and skates, skies and sleds, horseback and camels, surfboards and motorboats and boogey boards. Vehicles. All ways to move from here to there whether for seconds or minutes or hours or even days….the ride gave the rider something special for the journey.

It makes no difference who or what we are. Man or woman, child or adult, young or older, rich or poor, conservative or liberal, of faith or not, any town, any city, and any country.….vehicles move us, take us here and there and deliver us to where we want or need to go. Vehicles take us some place almost every single day. Vehicles take us to new places and new adventures, new challenges, and afford us the opportunity to see magnificent vistas up close or a bird's eye view of incredible landscapes. A voyage on a ship lets us see things like whales and dolphins and some incredibly large waves.

As wonderful and useful and rewarding as all that is, we have to understand that all vehicles have their own limitations. We can only travel if the vehicle is functioning properly. We can travel only as far as the amount of fuel in the vehicle allows. We can only use some of those vehicles if we know how to operate them since they are not all the same. Weather conditions can sometimes slow or prevent our travels. One very important limitation that all vehicles have is that regardless of how efficient or perfect or wonderful a vehicle is and in spite of all wonderful things those vehicles allow us to see and do, there is one place none of them can take us. Nobody can drive to Heaven. We will never sail to Heaven. You and I will never board any aircraft and fly there and it is a virtual guarantee there is not now, nor will there ever be, any model of rocket ship that will successfully get anyone to Heaven. There is only one vehicle that can take us all the way to God's home and it's the same ride everyone must take if they really want to go. Jesus! Jesus is the way. Did you see the Scripture at the top of the page? Let me reiterate. "…No one comes to the Father except through Me." **No One**. That's non-negotiable. That condition never changes. That rule applies to every single human being, past, present and future. God plays no favorites, nor does He make exceptions. The one and only way anyone ever gets to Heaven is through Jesus Christ. How does one do that? Simple. Believe in Jesus – sincerely. Go into a real relationship with Him. Accept Him as your Lord and Savior. That's it. It's free. But it's also the hardest, easiest thing anyone will ever do because coming to know and having a relationship with the King of Kings and Lord of Lords will change a person. For the better, to be sure, but you are going to change.

Now, don't let that scare you because if you thought motorcycles, skateboards, snowboards, motorboats and the luge were challenging, fun and exciting, I invite you to take a better ride. If you love excitement, adventure, challenge and having your thoughts provoked, your mind expanded and your heart perked to the max and riding the ultimate ride of your life, climb aboard the "Christ Express!" Let Jesus be your Conductor. This is a ride, no, *the* ride, I guarantee you, that can get you to Heaven. It's the only ride that can. Where was it you wanted to go today? How will you get there? Jesus – a life ride you gotta believe to go on. Travel well, today, Friend.

"This is the day the Lord has made! Rejoice! And be glad in it!" Do you hear that engine purr? That's God's love for you. Now you get out there and make this a Power Day!

Matthew 14: 28-30, "Lord, if it's you," Peter replied, "tell me to come to you on the water." "Come, He said." Then Peter got down out of the boat, walked on the water and came toward Jesus. But when he saw the wind, he was afraid and, beginning to sink, cried out, "Lord, save me!"

We've seen it happen to others and often. It is not only possible, but likely, this has happened to the person we see staring back at us in the mirror. It's the times when someone is so close to achieving their goal and for some reason, at the last moment, they heave a sigh, and quit. They stop one foot from the goal line. That one last rim of the basket is just too small. It is the one more "no" that somehow prevents a dream from becoming reality. One drop of water in the pipe and rust begins to corrode the entire system. Albert Schweitzer once observed that the saddest thing in life is that precious hope and motivation just dies inside a person long before his life does. The final straw – you know, the one that broke the camel's back. Obstacles wear us down, don't they? We get tired and irritated and angry until we finally throw our hands up in disgust and despair and say, "Enough! I've had it!!" It is all those pesky little things that take our focus off the goal. The distractions that nag us and drive us off course. The things that make us lose our focus.

The irony - the funny thing is - if we are truly focused on our goal, we don't actually notice those obstacles. Being focused is so intense that literally all attention is on the one task, the one goal, the one issue to be worked on right now to the total exclusion of all else. Have you ever been so focused that you don't even notice the clock or other people or the barking dog or the phone ringing right next to you or the approaching danger? Nothing gets in the way. At that moment, there is nothing else but the task at hand. For something to take that focus away at a critical time and cause you to stop altogether, it would have to be a very powerful thing. What could be so powerful to interrupt your focus and cause you to drop like rock….like Peter…..into the abyss? Doubt can do that. Fear is a more likely contender. Lies rank right up there along with guilt and condemnation. Such things invade your mind and will get in your way and before you realize what hit you, you're sinking fast.

Peter walked across the water toward Jesus with no problem at all. He was laser focused on the Lord. But then, Peter's peripheral vision locked onto the wind and a wave. A big wave distracted him and he got scared. Fear jumped on our buddy, Pete, forceing him to take his eyes off the Lord. Peter loses his focus and swoosh! He's getting dunked and yelling for help. Of course, Jesus is right there, as Jesus always is for any believer. Jesus is calm, collected, has it all going on and His focus is unshakable. Jesus reaches down, grabs Peter by the hand and saves him.

Hmmm…what's that? Has it happened to you? Have you had an internal conversation that sounds a lot like: "I lost focus, got distracted, the enemy took advantage and I fell. But I haven't called out to God for help, and now it's like I'm drowning in this huge mess."

We all have problems. No one is immune to them. But so far, you're silent. What are you waiting for? Remember in James, the half-brother of our Lord reminds us that "you have not because you ask not." God's just waiting for you participate in your own recovery. Ask for help! Perhaps you're afraid others might mock your pain. Does it embarrass you to find out you're as human as everyone else and finally realized there are trials you can't handle alone? Is it tough to admit you need God and to let His people help the great and powerful 'You'? Humble yourself. Amazing things happen when we admit we need help and can't do it all alone. The moment we do that, help starts showing up from places we never knew existed.

Call out to God, Friend. Get His help. We all have troubles and trials we face EVERY day! Jesus SAVES! 9-1-1 = Jesus. Copy Peter and call out, "Lord, help me!" And then….here's the hard part….trust Him to do that. Let Him help you. You have His written, irrevocable guarantee that He will keep His word. He'll help you refocus on your goal and move on to victory.

"This is the day the Lord has made! Rejoice! And be glad in it!" It is very comforting and definitely empowering to know that God will help you through whatever it is and that good bit of news should be more than enough for you to get out there and make this a Power Day!

Isaiah 43:16, "This is what the Lord says – He who made a way through the sea, a path through the mighty waters, …."

Let's take a short trek back in time to the days of Moses. The Israelites were getting out of Egypt. They had left their captors behind and were heading for a new home, about which they knew only that it was God's Promised Land, when they came to what any reasonable person would say was a rather significant obstacle. Perhaps you would agree that a body of water large enough to be labeled a "sea" would constitute a rather significant obstacle. To complicate matters further, the travelers are on foot; they are carrying all of whatever their worldly belongings were; they have no materials with which to build a boat and even if they had such materials, there was definitely nowhere near enough time to build a boat large enough to save all of them. The question arose: how does one manage to get a few million people across this watery obstacle while the world's largest army of bad guys chasing you is getting closer every minute? Yep, that would qualify as a problem. Big obstacle. Very little time. Very limited resources. What to do?

Their options were, shall we say, limited. Did they stand there waiting for a cruise ship to come by and pick them up? No. What did they have? They had Moses to lead them. They had listened to him and so far, things had gone okay. They were beginning to trust Moses because he seemed to have a connection with God so that was a plus. Moses was the kind of man given to sincere prayer so Moses did what he knew to do….he prayed. God answered him and gave Moses some instructions. The Bible tells us Moses obeyed God…(did you catch that? Moses _obeyed_ God….that's key… Moving on…) and followed God's instructions. Moses lifted his arms and God caused a mighty wind to blow. The wind blew so hard, so fast, so powerfully that it actually parted that huge body of water known as the Red Sea. And a few million Israelites, with all their stuff and all their livestock, WALKED across the floor of the Red Sea on dry land! God made a path *through* the sea. Kindly notice: the operative words here are *God made a path through…*

Okay. Nice story. So what? So, Dad/Mom/Manager person/CEO/Supervisor/ Wife-Husband/person facing a crisis….you have a major obstacle facing you and your time is short and resources are scarce and others are depending and relying on you to help them stay alive or employed or safe or provided for or fed! What do you do? So, there's a lesson for all of us in this story – which is more than just a lesson, it's the moral of the story. How does it get elevated from 'lesson' to 'moral'? By truth. This story is a historical account. It actually happened and that adds yet another amazing factor to the story. We will get to that in a moment. The lesson, the moral is this: Life has obstacles we have to face in every area of our lives. However, no matter what we have to face, no matter what is in front of us, even if it seems like the all-time, biggest problem we've ever encountered, it can be gotten *through*. The Israelites didn't engage in wishful thinking and wait for the kind of help that is supposed to magically arrive but never does. No, they looked to their leader, who set an example, prayed and obeyed, trusted God and went out *through* the sea (e.g. the problem) to get where they needed to be.

'Through.' That word keeps popping up, doesn't it? Notice, they didn't go around the problem. They didn't run away from the obstacle or try to go under it. To their great credit, they made no attempt to avoid the problem. They went *through* it.

Fast forward back to today. Maybe you're overwhelmed at work. Maybe your relationships are in turmoil. Could be strife is attacking you from one or more directions. Or, perhaps, you are just bone tired which serves to make that obstacle in front of you look insurmountable. Take heart. Look to your leader….to God your Father and pray. Then listen because He will give you directions. He might talk to you directly or He will send someone across your path who, "just happens" to tell you what you need to hear. Either way, when God gives you instructions, obey Him. Follow His instructions. We all have a written guarantee in the Word of God that we can and will make it if we are willing to simply Get God, Get Going, and Get Through!

"This is the day the Lord has made! Rejoice! And be glad in it!" Know that with God on your side and in your heart, how can you not smile? Today, get through and turn this into a Power Day!

Matthew 19:26, "But Jesus looked at them and said, 'With men this is impossible, but with God, all things are possible."

He stood at home plate and pointed towards the center field fence. The pitch is thrown, the ball speeding towards home plate at 90 miles per hour. Swoosh! The bat cuts the air as it misses its target. Strike One! The batter stepped back in the batter's box, adjusts his stance. He takes his time and once again, he points towards the center field fence. The pitcher winds up and lets the ball fly, zooming, hurtling towards its target. Another mighty swing and another miss! Strike Two! The noise coming from the crowd rises to ear-splitting levels as the batter, for a third time, raised his bat, pointing to the center field fence. Again, that baseball is flying at breakneck speed towards the catcher's glove. CRACK! The ball sails high into the air, easily covering the distance from home plate to the center field fence and beyond. It's a home run! Babe Ruth's home run record remained unbroken for decades but the thing most baseball fans will recall is that Babe Ruth did what they had previously believed to be impossible.

Hecklers chided Noah. Let's face it, from the perspective of those living through that time, it had to be hard not to say anything about what appeared to be something crazy happening. Here was this old man, who lived in a desert community, far from oceans, or seas or even a small lake, building a huge boat. Of course, God hadn't spoken to any of them, He had talked with Noah. Even so, they scoffed and mocked and doubted and claimed what Noah was doing was impossible.

Doubters scoffed at Eli Whitney's cotton gin. A machine that made it so much easier and faster to harvest cotton. Who knows how many laughed at the Wright Brothers? Must have been a lot of folks. "If God had wanted man to fly, He would have given us wings!" Imagine the many inventions and discoveries that have come about that faced ridicule, mockery and the jeers and taunting of skeptics and critics. All of them had the same message. "It's impossible. You're a fool to try. You'll only fail. Quit now. Go home!" People thought it impossible to have light bulbs, airplanes, alternating current, radios, televisions, cell phones and the list goes on.

Kindly notice that most of the things that were truly worth doing in this world were once labeled by the doubters as "impossible." The opposition must have been fierce and what the inventors endured to reach their goals must have been horrendous. It's a pattern that repeats itself still today. There are those who will claim something is impossible and say all sorts of negative, awful things….until someone comes along and does those things. We can count as our own blessing the fact that those who did the "impossible" things never paid much attention to the naysayers. Because they stuck to their guns, because they didn't give up on their dreams, we now have textiles, engines, fuel, medicines, technologies, and the million other things that you and I take for granted.

Once upon a time, someone told the person who tried it first to just give up because "it" would never work. Maybe that's happened to you. Someone saw what you were trying to do and their feedback was only gloom, doom and discouragement. Don't pay attention to that sort of talk. Listen, Friend, "… with God, *ALL* things are possible." (Emphasis added) What is it today that has you wondering whether or not it can be done? Pray about it. Put God in the middle of that thing and do it!

Proverbs 16:3, "Commit your activities to the Lord and your plans will be achieved." God will bless your efforts one way or another. Babe Ruth, Noah, Eli Whitney, Thomas Edison, Abe Lincoln, Rudy, Davy Crockett, Daniel Boone, so many others – they all did it, others did, people are still doing it, and you can, too! They exercise faith, believe, and get it done. "Go ye, therefore, and do ye likewise."

"This is the day the Lord has made. Rejoice and be glad in it." Smile, you Courageous Soul, you, and get out there and make this a Power Day!

Proverbs 3:5-6, "Trust in the Lord with all your heart and lean not on your own understanding: in all your ways acknowledge Him and He will direct your path."

There are days when it feels as though everything is caving in and trying to figure out which way to go or what to do first is nothing short of overwhelming. Perhaps you have had to change priorities because something more important suddenly inserted itself into your already busy schedule. Of course, there's the truly irritating scenario where you're all set to go, ready to tackle that major project and something happens that puts it on hold and now you have to wait. So, what do you do while you wait?

Then your memory recalls an old adage you've heard about picking your battles. You may even decide today is the day to start choosing what decision or project or person or trip or game or ____ gets to go first. Every now and then, I'll look at my schedule and know it's time to decide which battles to fight or avoid. It seems no sooner does that thought cross my mind, than I find myself embroiled in a confrontation over something unexpected that makes no sense whatsoever. If we're willing to admit it, many of us experience that. We so easily allow ourselves to get involved in battles we think are important at the time, that we end up fighting ourselves and alienating our allies. We become our own worst enemy. Too often we end up going to war over trivial things, making mountains out of mole hills, expending unnecessary emotional energy and wasting incredible amounts of our precious time as if no issue is too small. Then we're lost, overwhelmed, exhausted, and the last thing we know is which way to go or what to do next.

Lots of people unwittingly participate in stress collection. They'll charge into battles they didn't evaluate or think about, the ever-attractive lost cause. Having done so, they become more stressed, more confused, and more lost than before. Still, they will somehow find the strength and will to take on yet another cause and throw themselves on the tracks in vain attempts to stop the *reality* train. The only thing accomplished is finding themselves on the fast track to total burn out.

We have a society today full of burned-out employees; families led by burned out parents; marriages crumbling as burned-out spouses neglect each other;

and those who were once enthusiastic, dedicated, on-fire for Christ are now burned-out Christians. They thought they could handle it and took on more and more until they folded under the weight of all that stress. My Friends – none of it is worth it.

Consider again the wisdom of the adage to pick your battles. Pick winnable battles that matter. **Psalm 112:5** reminds us that "a good man will guide his affairs with discretion." More to the point, if you're not sure whether you should get involved in a particular battle or situation, "Trust in the Lord…. lean not on your own understanding."

Take a moment to think about those words. "Guide, Trust, Pick…." Each of those words imply the action is deliberate. It's a conscious act of your will. Look at your list of "battles" and ask yourself first how important is this one? Does it really matter? If the honest answer comes back, "not much" or "not at all" – then walk away from it. Will this affect my life or the lives of my family in a material way? If not, you may not need to mess with it right now or at all. Take it off the list or put it on the list of "Things to Get to Someday."

Of course, there are issues that must be faced now and we with which we must do battle. But if you take a breath, relax, go through the process of guiding your affairs with discretion, picking the battles that matter and ones you can win, trusting God, leaning on His wisdom, your battles will be fewer and you stress, much less.

"This is the day the Lord has made. Rejoice! And be glad in it!" Smile - now you have more time available since you're not fighting worthless battles. Use that time to make this a Power Day!

NOTES

1 Corinthians 9:24: "Do you not know that in a race all the runners run, but only one gets the prize? Run in such a way as to get the prize."

There are those who just hate competition either for themselves or their children or both. And if they hate it, then, by default, everybody else should feel the same way. Hence the unfortunate advent of "Participation Trophies." Heaven forfend anyone should feel even the slightest bit put out because they didn't win something. Winning a prize simply for showing up is disingenuous. Perhaps you might recall the days when the prize and trophy was awarded to First Place while those coming in second and third got a ribbon. Every other competitor had to bite the bullet, return to the practice field to work more, strive to improve, and prepare to compete another day. Why? Because "only one gets the prize."

Despite the best efforts of some to destroy healthy competition in most any area of life, we still benefit from life in a competitive society. Competition helps us get stronger, to learn more, to brave the unknown and untried in order to reach greater goals outside our comfort zones. Competition is good for everyone as it demands we throw off the bonds of mediocrity and embrace constant improvement. The big win for the favorite team or individual athlete was great but reality dictates that last week's win cannot and does not guarantee a win this week. The player or the team must start training again for next week's competition. More training and preparation are required because in the world of competition, any participant is only as good as their last performance. Work hard, play hard, excel, win, repeat. In the eyes of the world, only winners get the glory, and we all want to be the one wearing the Gold medal. In the world…..but God' race is different.

God's race - well, this race is far simpler but it's never easy. God's race is more challenging, lasting far longer. God's race takes an entire lifetime. The path on which the Christians run is rarely flat or oval. Rather, this path leads us on a tour through life that includes amazing victories, devastating defeats, lessons you never dreamed of learning, great joy and the experience of sorrow. God's race allows you to meet many personalities who can help you or hurt you and to know how to tell the difference. This race never lets you stay in your comfort zone very long because your comfort zone is not where the prizes are available. In this race, you never find your personal limits because no sooner will you reach what you thought was your limit, than a new experience comes along and takes you even further, surprising you again at what you really can accomplish. Occasionally, God's race will lead you directly through the Valley of the Shadow of Death where you are reminded of how much you really need a Lord and Savior and experience the true joy of knowing you are never alone in this race.

It's a hard race and many fall away. The good news is that even when you fall *down*, you don't have to fall *away*. God is always there to help you get back up and run some more. Here's the best news: it makes no difference at all in what order you finish. It only matters that you finish. Everyone who crosses that finish line – be they running, walking, or crawling – they finish the race by giving it their all for Christ and they win! The only losers are those who just plain quit and abandon the track. It's not a participation trophy since you did so much more than just show up or play in only one brief moment. You did what it took to finish. You "ran in such a way as to win the prize."

Sometimes it's fun to compete in the world. Sometimes it's a challenge. Sometimes the competition is harsh, seemingly not worth it at all. Sometimes you don't even want to be in that game. More good news! Run so as to get the prize of eternal life and don't worry about winning in the world. Simply focus on the finish line God laid out for you and the world will notice. Hoo boy, will they ever notice!

"This is the day the Lord has made. Rejoice! And be glad in it." Take heart, Godly athlete. You're running a great race! Keep going and do your part to run well and make this a Power Day!

1 **Thessalonians 4:1:** "Finally, brothers, we instructed you how to live in order to please God, as in fact you are living. Now we ask you and urge you in the Lord Jesus to do this more and more."

Notice something important here. According to Paul, the Thessalonians were not only taught how to live in order to please God...they were doing it! They were obviously doing it well because Paul's urged them to do more of it. Increase the intensity. Take it to the next level. This reminds us what James tells us, "*do not just read the Word, do what it says.*" **James 1:22**

This whole idea begs these questions: When we look in a mirror, finding and exercising the courage to ask this directly of ourselves, what is our honest answer? Are you living in a manner in which your primary purpose is first and foremost to please God? Oh, but the Thessalonians were instructed in how to do this properly! Yes, but you are, too. When you go to church and hear your pastor teach and preach, that's instruction. You should be reading God's word for yourself...if that's not instruction, what is? Maybe you go to Sunday School classes, Bible study groups, conferences, seminars, read books, fellowship....all are forms of instruction. The excuse of not getting any instruction bites the dust. See, if you really want to know how to live for Christ, do these things. Remember, once you know the truth, you are personally responsible for it so wisdom dictates you learn as much as you can and practice, practice, practice.

God tells us in His word, "This is love for God: to obey His commands." **1 John 5:3** Makes sense. If we claim to love God and believe in Him, logic demands we follow what He says. If we don't do that, somebody's playing the wrong game in a bad way. If we are living for God and we know that we know we are doing so...(not perfectly, of course....there's always room to grow) then the question becomes, "How can I do it better?" "What can I do to take it to the next level?" That will translate to be slightly different for each of us, but the goal is identical. Grow even closer to God. Build an ever-stronger relationship with Him and allow that to manifest in your life by living for Him.

Do what you've been doing...but more of it. Go deeper. Mind you...and this is important so get this...do not simply fill your time with busy stuff just to claim you're growing. Actually grow. Don't do something simply to check it off your list of "Got To Do This For Jesus" things. That's just "works" making the effort meaningless. Whatever you find to do to live more for God to please Him, make it worthwhile. It can be small or huge or time consuming or hardly take any time at all. That's not what counts. What counts is your heart. What counts is keeping God's commands. **1 Corinthians 7:19.** Not because you have to but because you truly want to.

So today - however that looks to you and whatever it means to you - are you living to please God? How can you do it more? More intensely? More often? More lovingly? More heartfelt? More worshipfully? Ask God. Listen to His answer. Do that.

"This is the day the Lord has made. Rejoice! And be glad in it." Smile - Living to please God is a challenge that brings immeasurable rewards. Now get out there and make this a Power Day.

Matthew 20:26-28: "...whoever wants to become great among you must be your servant, and whoever wants to be first must be your slave - just as the Son of Man did not come to be served, but to serve, and to give His life as a ransom for many."

To all you Vets out there, from our hearts, thank you! To all of you who continue to serve on active duty, in the Guard, or in the reserves, we thank you! We honor you and appreciate your selfless contributions to protect our nation, our freedom, our rights, and our liberty. All of you who served in the past and all of you who serve today; because of your service and sacrifices, you are truly the great and the first among us. Deservedly so. Thank you also to everyone who served behind the lines in the many support positions. Without you, those on the front lines could not have been successful in their efforts. Thank you! To all the families of uniformed service men and women who prayed and hoped and volunteered in myriad ways to ensure the troops and their families were well looked after and had what they needed in tough times....thank you! You are all worthy of the honor that comes from service.

We know only too well that when one spouse deploys to the battlefield, the other has a vital job at home and kids to care for. Someone has to supply the uniforms and the equipment. Supplies have to get to the troops. Somebody sets up communication systems making it possible for a Troop to call home. Somebody somewhere donates something for a care package. Others collect all those donations, put it together, organize it and ensure it gets delivered into the hands of a Soldier, Marine, Airman or Sailor they never met so that person can enjoy a moment and know that someone back home actually cares. Servants make that happen. Thank you. This is what Jesus refers to as slavery. Putting others ahead of self. Sacrificing your comfort so others can know theirs. Giving up what "I" want so that "you" can be better off. Service. It is greatness. This sort of slavery puts you first in line. Soldiers, Marines, Sailors, Airmen, Coast Guard, National Guard, and Reserves. They are giving it all so the rest of us can be comfy and warm and safe and peaceful.

Today, and indeed, any day, I challenge you to do something special to honor a veteran and/or any active-duty troop you run into. Let them go first in line. Pay for their lunch. Send a card through Blue Star Moms to a troop. Volunteer to do something to help. Reach out to a military family who needs some help and fill a need they might have. Tell them "thank you." Pray for them daily. RESPECT THEM. Give a veteran a job! Thank you, Veterans! Thank you, Active-Duty Troops! God bless you!

"This is the day the Lord has made. Rejoice! And be glad in it." Smile - They gave it all. They give it all. We benefit from their service. They deserve our respect. Now get out there and make this day a Power Day.

Being judgmental wrongly lets us think we have the right to change someone else. We never have that right. We only have the right to decide how we might change our own thoughts and actions. We must trust others to make their own choices and hold them accountable for the results of their choices. **Jeffrey D. Hill**

As a parent, have you ever found yourself thinking, "I have the right - and maybe even the duty - to change my kids!" Yeah...maybe. You certainly can, and should, affect their behavior and exert a lot of influence. Maybe you look at your own family and think "this is a whole 'nother story." For now, let's just focus on those we connect with outside our immediate family.

Here's a bottom-line truth we all need to understand and accept: God created each of us. Everyone we see – no matter where and regardless of who they are or what they're doing or saying, whether we ever meet them or not, is God's handiwork. We can't change God's handiwork. Only God can do that. The individual must want to accept that change and he or she must be a voluntary, willing participant. You and I do not have the power, the expertise, and certainly not the right to change anyone except ourselves. We can only change ourselves with God's help.

We can choose how we think. We can choose how we feel. We can choose how we behave or believe or simply be. We can change ourselves - or not - as we see fit. Our free will extends all the way to the end of our own self and not one inch further. If John Doe does something you disagree with, for example, it's John Doe's responsibility, not yours, simply because you didn't do whatever he did. It's not up to you to change John Doe's mind or heart, but you can plant a seed. How? By being a good influence. You can speak into his life with words of wisdom, encouragement, hope and love. There's never a wrong time to set a good example. You can also choose how you react to John Doe and if that wasn't your best effort, you can work on changing how you react to such occurrences. Or not.... that's your choice, too. But the fact is, you're not going to change John Doe.

When you plant a seed, God takes it from there. God goes to work on the soil in John's life and it is God who makes it possible for the seed you planted to grow. If John is willing, change happens. For example: Writing to Senators and Representatives is highly effective in getting certain issues noticed and acted upon. Short, concise letters highlighting three main points tend to get the point across very well. Write both to those you support and those whose opinion differs greatly. They may or may not ever respond and it's guaranteed a staffer is the one reading your letter and passing along its content. But now they know how you feel about a given issue and understand if you feel that way, most likely many others feel the same way. Even if you don't write letters or send emails, you can still hold them accountable with your vote which is also effective. Put the responsibility for their actions on their shoulders, where it rightly belongs, and hold them accountable. You know what happens then? Results. It may not change their character or thinking so much...but the results are of great value.

God does likewise with all of us. Other people rightly do likewise with us. Why? It works. Judgmentalism never works. You'll only get frustrated. Give credit where it's due and hold people responsible for what is properly theirs to bear.

"This is the day the Lord has made. Rejoice and be glad in it." Smile - Lead by good example and you won't have to worry much about judging. Now get out there and make this a Power Day.

Isaiah 26:3 "You will keep in perfect peace him who mind is steadfast, because he trusts in you."

What does it mean to be steadfast? If one is steadfast, one is firmly fixed in faith and devotion to duty. To be steadfast is to be constant and unchanging. In a word, one who is steadfast is faithful. Loyal. Dependable. Dedicated. Trustworthy. All these words well describe one who is steadfast.

God is steadfast and perfect in His love and grace to us and has proven it time and again. When we are likewise devoted to Him, He honors that; He will "keep in perfect peace" such a person. Does that mean a devoted believer can skip through all their days under blues skies, enjoying tranquility and the fresh scent of roses, free of challenge or trial? Not by a long shot. It is, however, quite possible to remain in "perfect peace" and while going through any of life's very difficult challenges. True story.

It's a good bet there are people in your own life about whom you might wonder how they can be inundated with so many tough issues in their lives but others would never know it because these folks behave like they still have it all securely together. And the fascinating thing is - they really do. Such a person, I'm willing to bet, has a very close relationship with God.

I do not wish to sound like this is bragging in any way, because it's not. In this, full credit and glory goes only to God. Here's a direct quote from "The Detroit News" dated Sunday, July 29, 1956 which was 4 days after the sinking of the Andrea Doria. The Andrea Doria was an Italian ocean liner on which my family were passengers. "The Hills were one of the most composed and happiest families among those rescued." That quote was mostly about my parents and my older brother and sister. I was only four at the time and my two younger brothers were two months old. Why would my folks be that composed after going through a shipwreck which could have killed us all? Simple: Steadfast faith, trust and love for a steadfast God. My dad was asked how he managed to get us all off safely. He said he had no idea and looked toward heaven.

My dad and my brother, Eric, did heroic things on that ship without ever thinking they were doing heroic things. My dad just did them because it was the right thing to do, and Eric helped him because dad said so. Steadfast faith and trust. My father said....my brother obeyed. My father obeyed because his Father said so. My mother stayed strong and calm and seemingly fearless just because she knew God was nearby. The first thing she told us children to do when we were awake enough to grasp her command was to pray. We did. Because she was calm and strong, so were we. Because God was steadfast, so was mom. And today, it's a tiny, obscure piece of history to be known as a member of "one of the most composed and happiest families..." in the middle of a crisis. My parents, and by extension, we kids didn't do that. God did that. He did it for my parents and He'll do it for you and yours and anyone who trusts Him. God is steadfast so you can be also. Today, walk firmly fixed in your faith.

"This is the day the Lord has made. Rejoice! And be glad in it." Smile - "The steadfast love of the Lord never ceases." Don't let yours, either. Now get out there and this a Power Day.

NOTES

Something To Ponder:

"Correction does much, but encouragement does more." **Goethe**

Despite what some may choose to believe, there is not one individual human who has ever, is now or will ever walk on this planet who is perfect – except Jesus the Christ. All the rest of us are flawed is some way and everyone makes mistakes from time to time. Some more often than others.

Of course, we do our best to avoid it but, the fact is, mistakes are inevitable. Most of them are unintentional. A lot of mistakes are born of our own ignorance while just as many result from not taking the time to fully think things through. One can easily find plenty of examples on YouTube or America's Funniest Videos, the news, and a host of other sources. Fact of life: everyone makes mistakes.

Mistakes are one of the core reasons there's a perpetual, real need for both forgiveness and correction. Consider a situation where a child or an employee does something wrong. They make a mistake. What good does it do to scold and criticize that person but invest no time at all teaching them how to avoid that mistake in the future? None, at all. How will they know what the right thing to do is if we don't teach them? This premise holds true in pretty much any situation or relationship.

Of course, there are times when difficult conversations are necessary. We can be careful and loving in our criticism, but it's truly unfair if we only tell someone how bad their mistake was. All that does is demoralize, and possibly demean the person while doing nothing to fix the problem or prevent it from being repeated. What does help is correction. Simply taking the short time necessary to impart the message, "Here's where you made a mistake, here's what you should have done and why you should have done it that way" is a huge help with great benefits. It protects the person's self-esteem, helps them grow and lets them know they are still valued.

Even more helpful and securing the lessons of correction while fostering real growth and improvement in a person is encouragement. It's one thing to point out a flaw. The person now feels bad....probably. It's a whole new thing to offer correction and possible solutions. The person will be more informed, even though he probably still feels bad. If you add to that a heartfelt bit of encouragement, now they will be highly motivated to excel the next time. Why? You just proved you care more about them than the mistake they made. They know you are not judging them permanently as a horrible person because of one mistake. They still have hope. Hope is very powerful.

Look at the differences: "You really messed this up! How could you do that?! Clean this mess up! I'm never giving you this job again!" That's just critical. This is devoid of any help or encouragement or correction. Add correction and some encouragement and the message sounds a lot like this: "John, that was a real mistake! Look at what happened! It would have been better if you had done it like this instead. It's okay, John, because I know you have what it takes to do this right. Rethink your methods and try again." This approach will do a lot more to help a person learn, learn it well and remember it, and they will actually want to do better.

Encouragement is an amazing thing. The Bible reminds us that those who encourage others will themselves be encouraged. Today is perfect day to look for opportunities to encourage your kids, your spouse, your subordinates, or employees and watch what happens. I think you'll be pleasantly surprised.

"This is the day the Lord has made. Rejoice! And be glad in it." Smile - It's one thing to teach...helping them learn is altogether something else. Now get out there and make this a Power Day.

Psalm 78:32: "In spite of all this, they kept on sinning; in spite of His wonders, they did not believe."

If we're to be completely honest with ourselves, we must admit there is one thing humankind the world over has in common. Something that has existed since time in memorial. It is one thing people have perfected to an art form. That thing is stupid behavior. People don't have to be stupid to do stupid things. Let's define 'stupid behavior' so we're on the same page. This is any behavior where the actor is foolish, inane, silly, bent on folly such as attempting a difficult task or act for which they have no skills or speaking with authority on a topic about which the speaker knows nothing. It is behavior that makes you shake your head in disbelief and wonder why anyone would ever do, or say, such a thing.

Proof is in such abundance that finding it requires little effort. Open any social media site and one is instantly faced with more stupidity than one can imagine. Look, for example, at any post related to a current political issue and the responses to that post. You find proof by way of deliberate, foolish, and frivolous comments in which the writer unwittingly shows the world their understanding of the topic is non-existent. It is a daily occurrence, and to be fair, no one is exempt. Open a video on YouTube and find that stupid behavior is not bound by age, gender, or socio-economic bracket. Everyone has the capacity for stupid behavior and sadly, way too many people freely prove it to the world with wild abandon.

Ancient Israelites mastered stupid behavior. How? Look at today's verse once again. It starts by saying, "In spite of all this…" That begs the question, "In spite of all what?" **Psalm 78** uses the first 30 verses to recap many of the wonderful, good, and miraculous things God had done for His people from the time He delivered them out of bondage until this Scripture was written and beyond. The Israelites were happy and overjoyed to be free – at first. However, human nature being what it is, it didn't take them long to start whining and complaining about – well, you name it. They complained about the food, the desert, the leadership, the heat, the cold, the noise, the silence, each other and so on. It's human nature. The stupidity? They had been freed from slavery, all their needs were provided for, but because the timing didn't meet their own expectations, they chose to wallow in self-pity.

God had finally heard enough of this and became upset. He decided it was time to teach them a lesson. Now, you'd think getting disciplined once would be enough and for many people, one time is more than sufficient, but not so with our ancient Israelites. They dove headlong into making a habit of acting like whiny crybabies and pitching fits until they got what they wanted. When they got it, they'd mumble a phony thank you and immediately revert to the same stupid behavior that got them into trouble in the first place! They turned it into an art form. God performed all manner of miracles in plain view, for their benefit, and they still didn't believe. These people did agree God was real and existed...but they worshipped idols, too. They were hedging their bets, so to speak, in case this whole "One true God thing" didn't pan out.

What's new about all this in our time? Nothing, except our idols are different. Think how this relates to your own life and tell me it isn't true. On Monday, we get an unexpected or long prayed-for blessing. We are joyous, thanking God profusely for it. We're sincere and genuinely happy. Tuesday dawns and something negative happens to us and you'd think we'd been victims for our entire life! We utter stupid phrases like, "Oh come on, God! Seriously? Why would God do this to me?! What did I do to deserve this?" We get caught in that trap with our kids, our spouses, our employers. One day it's, "Oh Sweetheart, you're so wonderful and I love you so much," in a heartbeat, what was so great is now so irritating. The job we have and the company we work for is a blessing we appreciate but when something goes wrong one time, the same mouth that sang those praises now spews vile things about that job. We do that with our new "toys" as soon as the new starts to wear off. "I got this awesome computer! It's the best thing in the whole world!" Three months later: "What's the matter with this stupid thing?! It is such junk!"

The problem is our memory. We forget all the good things and the joy they brought and how they blessed our life. "In spite of all that," we focus on the problems. We ignore the fact that the problems we encounter are, very often, *our own* fault. We keep on sinning, repenting, slip and slide and we keep having to ask God to forgive us....again and again. Today, you and I can begin to break that chain and start something better. Any time you're mad at God or anyone or anything else, ask yourself, "What has God done for me?"

Remember all those things. Then ask yourself, "What have I done for Him?" Then adjust *your* attitude and go on to a brighter day.

"This is the day the Lord has made. Rejoice! And be glad in it." Smile - Keeping God in your mind and heart does wonders for your whole life. Now get out there and make this a Power Day.

Matthew 9:28, 29: "...Do you believe I am able to do this? Yes, Lord, they replied. Then He touched their eyes and said, 'According to your faith will it be done to you....'"

Don't just skip over these words because they are powerful verses of Scripture. Its context is in a story of Jesus restoring the sight of two blind men. In the Bible, we find Jesus healing a lot of blind people. Some of the stories are repeats of an earlier event and others are separate occurrences, but He did this a lot. There is a unique thing, though, in this story that is an important lesson for us all.

Notice three important parts of these two verses. First, Jesus asks these two men if they believe. Believe what? That Jesus could heal their blindness. In other words, He asked if they had faith. Yes, they did. Okay, hold it right there These guys were blind, so they had obviously never seen Jesus or had a chance to see Him work miracles. How did they come to have faith that He could do this? They had heard about Him. "Faith comes by hearing..." **Romans 10:17** They heard, and they believed. They believed it so well they had no doubt whatsoever that Jesus was who He said He was, and He could do what had been said about Him. They were convicted and convinced.... belief – faith - is a powerful thing!

Second, who does the healing? Jesus, not the two men. God did the healing. But notice, He has them participate in their own healing by their faith. God isn't a supernatural ATM whom we go to whenever we need something. He will always ask us to do our part, however great or small. This is a relationship deal. We do what we can do, and God will do whatever we can't do. That's the deal. Need more proof? The Bible is full of instances where God tells us, "If you.......then, I will....." If you obey, if you go, if you do....then – get that - 'then' I will..." His part comes *AFTER* you do your part. That's why Jesus asked them first if they believed. They had to do something in order to be able to say yes. What did they do? They sacrificed all other previously held worldly notions and they believed. That's not an easy thing to do. It takes real effort and an unwavering desire to overcome old habits. Faith, amongst other things, does require action.

Third, Jesus told them how powerful their faith, in and through Him, really could be. He let them know how much control they really had in this deal. "According to *YOUR* faith, *WILL IT BE DONE...*" to whom? Themselves. Major Point: "According to your faith…" here is NOT a measure of how much faith these guys had. Quantity of faith makes no difference. It simply says, "Because you have faith…" God heals. God does the work. God performs the miracles, whether it's healing blind guys, parting a sea, walking on water or whatever. But the person to whom or for whom the work is accomplished *uses their faith* to move Jesus to do it. What if one of these guys said, "Well, I don't know if you can do it or not. I just came along to find out what my pal here was talking about." According to his faith, or lack of it, he'd still be blind. Remember, just a few verses earlier, the woman who bled constantly was in the same crowd as Jesus. As He passed by, she was able to just barely touch the hem of Christ's robe and she was instantly healed. That was faith. Jesus healed - "I felt power go out of me." - but it was "*your faith* has made you well." **(Mth 9:22, Mark 5:34)**

Christ didn't travel around performing miracles just to have something to do. He wasn't into parlor tricks. He never forced Himself or miracles on anyone who did not accept Him. He did these things mostly for believers and occasionally to help motivate people to become believers. But He was looking for cooperation from people. Faithful cooperation. It's a joint effort in which you believe, He does. Will He do everything you believe for? Nope. God is not a "sugar daddy"...He's God. He'll do all that is in line with His will and purpose for our life but He's not there to satisfy our every whim. Here's the takeaway: "according to your faith will it be done to you." *Your* faith. What *YOU* believe for. Don't let your faith limit you to settling for less than all God has for you. While it is wrong and greedy to abuse our faith for selfish reasons, it's not greed to want and believe for *everything* God has for you. It's your faith. Do with it what you will but if you want that abundant life Jesus went to a lot of trouble to make available to you, exercise your faith to the full and believe God can, and will, do it for you.

"This is the day the Lord has made. Rejoice! And be glad in it." Smile - Exercise your faith to the full then get out of God's way and let Him be God. Now get out there and make this a Power Day.

"Hard pressed on the right. My center is yielding. Impossible to maneuver. Situation excellent. I am attacking!"
General Ferdinand Foch, Battle of the Marne 1918

It was during the onslaught of invasions from Nazi Germany during World War II and while Great Britain stood resolute in opposition, Sir Winston Churchill pointed to the wisdom of attacking enemy airfields while the planes were still on the ground. Often under heavy attacks on their home turf, Britain's Air Forces nonetheless remained highly effective. Early on the morning of December 7,1941, Japan attacked the U.S. Naval base at Pearl Harbor, bombing our naval fleets and airfields. They managed to inflict incredible damage to our forces while they were at their point of departure. It took the U.S. a few years to build enough new ships and planes to mount an effective counter offensive.

If you study military warfare tactics, especially guerilla-type operations, you find this same principle of striking as close to home as possible is lavishly applied. During WWI, General Foch, the Supreme Commander of the Allied Forces faced an all-out onslaught from the enemy while his forces were in disparate straits. September 11, 2001, Islamic terrorists attacked us at home and caught us napping. The three hijacked planes had barely left the city their flights originated from. You can pick a war or a skirmish or any major successful battle and you'll find the victor rarely waited for the enemy to come to him. He took the fight to the enemy, at his home. Why is that? It works. Look at fighters who box or fight in MMA or the UFC. When the ref gives them the "Go" signal, the fighters run towards each other – taking the fight to the enemy.

When you review our history, it is hard not to notice that other than the Revolutionary and Civil Wars, the U.S. never fought a war on our own soil. We always take it to them and do everything possible to prevent the enemy from coming to us. It's much easier to defeat the enemy when the enemy is cornered on his own turf. It is so much harder to stay calm, focused and unemotional when one must defend his own land, property and loved ones. It's demoralizing and the defender is forced to fight the battle in a weakened state. Of course, there are exceptions to the rule....there always are. But most often, if you want to defend against any menace, the most effective tactic is to strike first, strike hard and catch them sleeping, while their forces are parked. Pearl Harbor is proof of how effective this tactic can be. It's the military version of "nip it in the bud."

Okay....so what? Are we at war? Is there danger of being attacked soon? Yes. But don't worry, it's only a threat every day. The threat we face does not come from enemy planes. The threat comes from the devil. Satan is the only enemy we have, though his tools and methods are legion. Every day he attacks our morals, our values, our families, our businesses, our schools, and anything and everything having to do with our belief in God. This enemy is attacking all of us, all the time, in some manner and he does it so skillfully that sometimes, we don't even notice. He's attacking in your house, through your eyes, in your mind, in your heart, in your children, in your relationships, in your workplace and always right at your weakest, least defended point.

So, what are we to do? First, take heart. **John 14:1** reminds us to "Let not your heart be troubled." We know Jesus also used this effective tactic when His spirit left the cross and made a beeline to Hell where Jesus conquered the enemy and death and successfully overcame the world. Second, the best and most powerful weapon we have is always freely, and abundantly available. Your best weapon is prayer. Use it as much and as often as you like. Third, you have a free will, courtesy of God Almighty, with which you have the power and might through your Lord and Savior Jesus Christ to say "No!" to whatever the devil throws at you. "Resist the devil and he will flee from you." **James 4:7** As history proves, resisting early – as in the moment your feet hit the floor every morning, prevents the devil from gaining a foothold. **Eph. 4:27** Start the day with prayer, resist the enemy, attack him by binding him away in Jesus' name, and don't even give him a chance. "Put on the full armor of God," **Eph. 6:13** then walk in victory from the very beginning of the day!

"This is the day the Lord has made. Rejoice and be glad in it." Smile - All big problems began as small ones. Solve the small ones fast so they can't get big. Now get out there and make this a Power Day.

Consider This: "A greedy man stirs up dissension but he who trusts in the Lord will prosper." **Proverbs 28:25**

We have all known a person whose focus in life is only on getting more and keeping it for themself. This is the greedy, aggressive person who is in business purely for selfish reasons. He or she has no concern whatsoever who they have to hurt or use, and they don't hesitate to do whatever they can to increase their power, line their own pockets and gratify themselves. That's not the sort of person God calls us to be. God call us to a higher standard.

Indeed, God wants us to use the gifts He gave us. That's why He gave us gifts. However, He wants us to use those gifts to serve others. The good news is that when we obey Him in that, we also are blessed. God wants us to prosper. His definition of prosperity is not what the world says it is. What He said is He gives us wealth so we can be generous to others - so we can sow seed. **(2Cor. 9:11)** We are supposed to use our wealth in the service of others. God calls us to be good stewards of wealth. We can be generous with the wealth of our time. We can be generous with the wealth of our skill. We can be generous with the wealth of our money. And we can always give more compassion.

When we open a business or excel at our jobs, our focus should never be "What's in this for me?" Our thoughts should not be on personal gain from doing our work, even though, we will grow and likely benefit because of our work. Our focus should be in trusting God to lead us on the paths we need to walk. We are to do good things for His glory and to serve others in some manner. When we do *that, then* we prosper. Repeatedly, in His word, God tells us that if we put Him first, trust Him, obey Him, listen to, and adopt His wisdom, and continue to do so as we pursue our lives, He will provide everything we need. The key, indeed, the prerequisite, is to trust Him first.

A pastor rightly reminded his congregation that for us to trust God, we must know Him. It's hard to trust someone we don't know. How do we get to know God? Simple: Read His word and meditate on it. Pray. Fellowship with other believers. Attend church and pay attention and learn the intricacies of God's love and will for us. The more you get to know Him and experience His presence, the more you'll come to trust Him. The more you trust Him, the more and better you can do what He needs and asks you to do. The more you do that, the more your faith matures and the greater your life abounds. Does that mean you get wildly rich with lots of cool stuff? Nope. There is never a guarantee of financial riches, but you will have the wealth money can never purchase. You will *prosper* by your trust in the Lord. That's what His word says and that will enrich your life in many good ways.

It's a process. Anything worthwhile takes time and effort and this is no different. Today, as you go to work and about your business, trust God to lead you. Whatever your situation or circumstance may be, focus on trusting God and let His example of good behavior take you where you need to be. Do all you do "as unto the Lord" and don't worry about anything else. Key point: prosperity may come in the form of financial wealth, or job security, or the number and types of friends or counselors we need, or in our relationships, or in personal safety, or in any of a thousand different ways. You'll easily recognize it because you'll realize that things "just happen" to begin improving. When that happens, give God the glory and your thanks because you obeyed, you trusted, and He kept His word. You prospered. Today, just trust God.

"This is the day the Lord has made. Rejoice! And be glad in it." Smile - Trust leads to prosperity, thankfulness leads to more...bottom line, it's all about putting God first in everything and giving Him our deepest respect. Now get out there and make this a Power Day.

NOTES

Psalm 118: 28, 29 "You are my God, and I will give you thanks; you are my God, and I will exalt you. Give thanks to the Lord, for He is good; His love endures forever."

If your experience growing up was anything like mine, you learned early on there was a two-word phrase you should never say to mom or dad. Uttering this brief phrase was a sure way of finding yourself doing a lot of things you didn't want to do. That phase is, "I'm bored."

Perhaps you find yourself with time on your hands and are wondering what you could do today that would be productive, helpful and worthwhile. May I suggest you take a quick moment to read the verses at the top of this page again....and then *do that*. It will surely cure any feelings of boredom you had.

The reason offered in Verse 29 should more than satisfy any curiosity as to why this is a good thing to do. Is that not a good way to spend some of your day...thanking God for all He's made possible in our lives? You have a whole day's worth of time to use for something. Use it to thank God for all He's done for you. You could do this all day and never run out of things to let Him know you're grateful for. Some time ago, my wife suggested we write down everything we were thankful for and I went along. At the time, my attitude was, admittedly, less than admirable so I grabbed a pen and a pad of little yellow sticky notes and used one sheet – one – to write down the few things I thought would suffice and then left the table. I returned about an hour later to find my wife had filled up much of a college-ruled, spiral notebook, front and back of each page with a never-ending list of things for which she wanted to thank God. And she wasn't finished. She kept going. When I saw her list, I learned this lesson.

You can waste your time if you like. You don't have to rush anywhere...unless you just want to. You can take a nap if you like. You can play with the kids or take your wife, husband or that special someone on a date to spend time together and enjoy build the relationship. While you do any or all of that, look around at where you are and what surrounds you and make a deliberate decision to begin thanking God for all the things that positively impact your life.

It is quite surprising what that will do for your spirit and attitude. Take a close look at your kids and be thankful. Consider your job and your purpose...and be thankful. Look at the car you drive and house you live in and be thankful. Gaze at your spouse and recall why you fell in love with that person and exalt God for bringing love into your life. Then realize how incredibly rich you really are...and be thankful. Any day of the week, any time, regardless of where you are, it's a good day and time and a perfect place to soak up His word and get fed on Truth, exalt God your Father....and be thankful. Now, let me be bold and claim that doing this will prove to be a great way to invest in your family, in your life, and your eternity. Thankfulness is a huge deal in the eyes of God. Practice it all the time.

"This is the day the Lord has made. Rejoice and be glad in it." Smile and get out there and make this a Power Day.

1 Corinthians 3:16-17: "Don't you know that you yourselves are God's temple and that God's Spirit lives in you? If anyone destroys God's temple, God will destroy him; for God's temple is sacred, and you are that temple."

Perhaps you read that passage and immediately thought it's talking about eating right, exercise, and staying in shape. It might be easy to reach that conclusion and we could apply good thoughts and lessons to it. Indeed, there's nothing wrong with that and it certainly never hurts to stay healthy and in shape since we are, in fact, God's temple and should be excellent stewards of it.

However, that's not what Paul was talking about here. In its proper context, Paul was talking about divisions in the church – which is the body of Christ - the temple of God. When Paul wrote this, it was those on *Team Apollos* pitting themselves against *"Team Apostle Paul.* It was then, the battles raged over doctrinal issues and processes and man-made rules and ideas about how one is to be a "real Christian." It isn't too much different today in too many places. We still hear arguments like, "You can't be a real Christian unless you pray this way or worship that way or believe this thing or that." The responses come back like, "Oh Yea?! Well, you're not a true Christian because you sprinkle instead of dunk and you use grape juice instead of wine for communion." Churches get so tangled in this arrogant, prideful nonsense they forget they're just one part of *THE* church and maybe all they're doing is upsetting Jesus. Man doesn't make the rules. God does and His rules are the only ones that matter. Nonsense within competing denominations who pick away at petty differences until they fester and grow into major rifts ultimately works to destroy God's temple. That's the warning Paul was giving here. So, with love and in the spirit of unity for God's church, STOP THAT!

If you're a parent of multiple children, you've no doubt had occasion to give your children a toy or a game to share. In short order the children are squabbling over how to play or whose turn it is or *they* didn't do it right or any one of a hundred other things. Remember your reaction? It probably sounded something like "HEY! If you can't play nice with that, NO ONE will get to play at all and all of you will be punished!" 'Punished' in my house meant they would sit in time out for as long as I was in the mood for peace and quiet - which was sometimes too long as noted by my wife asking, "Where are the kids?" Oops.....

"Different" doesn't necessarily mean "wrong." Mostly, it's just different. Regardless of Christian denominations,(which are not mentioned in the Bible at all), all Christians are called to get along. So what if they do "X" differently than how you're used to? It doesn't mean they're automatically doomed to eternal fire and torment. In our nation, we have all sorts of diversity, some of which are, in fact, outside of God's will but that's for God to manage. A great thing about our country is how we celebrate the individual and differences. It's wrong to think we have to hate anyone with whom we don't agree. We can still be friends without liking, condoning or supporting each other in some beliefs or activities. Still, we are all Americans who form ONE nation. If we constantly pick each other apart over little issues eventually, those wounds become serious. They fester and the temple is destroyed. Doctor Edwin Cole, in a speech he shared at a Promise Keepers rally in Tulsa, OK back in the late 90's asked all of the men attending this question: "Are you a Catholic, or are you Christian? Are you a Methodist, or are you Christian? Are you a Baptist or Episcopalian or are you Christian?" Christians follow Christ in His way. Denominations tend to follow Christ "His way" filtered through their own man-made rules. That's a problem causing division in the Kingdom.

<u>"Jesus knew their thoughts and said to them, 'Every kingdom divided against itself will be ruined, and every city or household divided against itself will not stand."</u> **Mth 12:25**. It's great to stand up for God and what we believe in but remember, the goal is to edify, build up, restore, enhance, and grow God's kingdom, not destroy His temple.

"This is the day the Lord has made. Rejoice and be glad in it." Smile - If we were all exactly alike, we wouldn't need understanding or cooperation. We're all individuals....and God's temple. Now get out there and make this a Power Day.

Proverbs 4:14,15: "Do not set foot on the path of the wicked or walk in the way of evil men. Avoid it, do not travel on it; turn from it and go on your way."

If you're older than 4, you may already know why this advice from Proverbs is spot on and worthy of our attention. Going down the wrong path only leads to all sorts of trouble. And that is true 100% of the time.

Recall the last time you were tempted to do anything you knew from the get-go was a bad idea but, at the time, you chose to do it anyway. It doesn't matter what it was. Do you have that image in your mind? Okay, so, how did that turn out for you? At the very least you probably felt pangs of guilt. Maybe you got caught. Maybe in doing that thing, you managed to make someone you care about very mad or worse; they let you know they were disappointed in you. That's why God, through His word in this proverb, warns us..."Don't go there! It's the wrong way! It will not turn out well if you do! Go this other way, instead!" God isn't being mean or controlling, He wants to help you have a better life!

We all have better choices available to us and wisdom simply dictates that we pick one of those, instead. The children of loving, caring parents learn this lesson well when they're young. Just like those young children, though, we adults will test God to see just how far we can go before He lets us know we've arrived at "Far Enough!" Too often, we have to re-learn not to hop on the bus for a ride to "Too Far." That's a nasty neighborhood and while getting there is quite easy, leaving that dangerous place is never easy or fast. Make no mistake, the path leading to wickedness and the way of evil looks really fun and enticing because, well, it can be! But that's Satan's deception. The truth is that bit of fun will cost far more than you bargained for and the payback required is often something we cannot afford.

This verse and the warning it provides recalls a scene from the movie, *Karate Kid 2*. In this scene, Mr. Miyagi employs an object lesson to teach Daniel a valuable lesson. The master sets up a large hook on a block and tackle type device, so it would swing like a pendulum. He shows Daniel how to dodge properly and instructs him by saying, "Best defense: Don't be there." Then, Miyagi lets go of the hook which swings swiftly directly towards Daniel. If

Dan had not moved - had he stayed put - he would have been skewered. Avoid that path. You can see it coming. Don't be there.

We all face temptation to walk the wrong paths and indulge in the wrong ways. It is to our advantage to employ the lesson: Your best defense is to not even go there in the first place. "Avoid it, do not travel on it; turn from it and go on your way." Today, and every day, deliberately avoid the hook. Don't be there. Look at your more worthy options and make better choices.

"This is the day the Lord has made. Rejoice! And be glad in it." Smile - Truth is, God's way is always better, even more fun and far more exciting. Go His way. Now get out there and make this a Power Day.

Something to Ponder:

"It is pleasing to God whenever thou rejoicest or laughest from the bottom of thy heart." **Martin Luther**

The verses found in Scripture that talk about rejoicing tell us rejoicing in God is good for our soul. For example: **Isaiah 61:10,** says in part, "…my soul rejoices in my God." Also, **Luke 1:47** tells us, "And Mary said, 'My soul glorifies the Lord and my spirit rejoices in God my Savior'…" God talks about laughing at the wicked and at evil. He also says in **Eccl. 3:4** that "there is a time to weep and a time to laugh." That's highly encouraging. I don't know about you, but I do love a good laugh!

Even more, I love rejoicing with others over the things God does in their lives. Like when a friend who was praying for healing from a serious illness went back to the doctor for a check-up and is told that *"somehow"* the tests show it's suddenly as if that person never even had that disease. Because that actually happened, we can honestly say that answered prayer is always a cause to rejoice!

Laughter and rejoicing. Various researchers have studied in depth the effects of these on people and all indications are that laughter and rejoicing lead to greater happiness and better health. We have proof these are good things to do. Martin Luther, *the* Point Man in the Reformation, believed it pleases God when we are genuinely happy and able to laugh about things and rejoice over life. I agree. God sent His Son so that we can have an abundant life. How is that not worth rejoicing over?

Whenever the devil and his ugly henchmen get humiliated in some fashion is always good for a laugh. Like when a teenaged kid named David helped a nasty giant get stoned – okay, that was hokey but ha, ha anyway. How about that time Satan tried to wipe out Christianity by killing Jesus on a cross? We all know who still to this day gets the last laugh on that one. There are so many ways life can be just plain fun, too. Sharing fun moments is a worthy way to rejoice. Whether you're doing something outdoors with family and friends or playing board games indoors or just spending time together, it is good for your soul. Laughing has a way of cleaning out all the cobwebs of doubt, fear and frustration and allowing your body to heal from stress. God has made this world a really fun and funny place and you don't have to go far to find something to laugh about or rejoice in if you just look.

Today, short and sweet and simple: Rejoice. Rejoice in a sunrise or sunset. Rejoice in your family or your job or the myriad little things that happen throughout the day to remind you that God wants you to enjoy life. Laugh! There are so many things to find good humor in. For example, the actual warning label on one brand of clothes iron says this, "Do not iron clothes on body." You have to wonder what that certain someone was thinking when he or she tried...come on....that's funny! The label on a shower cap box says the item inside "Fits one head." Do you really need to tell people that? Look on a box of Swans *__frozen__* dinners and you may find this: Are you ready? Here it comes...this is for real: "Serving Suggestion: Defrost." Okay, there are college-educated, management level people who get paid big bucks to think this stuff up and make us all wonder whatever happened to common sense! Tell me God doesn't have a great sense of humor! Rejoice! Laugh! God loves it when your heart is jolly. Today, let your heart smile.

"This is the day the Lord has made. REJOICE! And be glad in it." Smile - no, really....smile. Now get out there and make this a Power Day.

Hebrews 12: 1-3: "Therefore, since we are surrounded by such a great cloud of witnesses, let us throw off everything that hinders and the sin that so easily entangles, and let us run with perseverance the race marked out for us. Let us fix our eyes on Jesus, the author and perfecter of our faith, who for the joy set before Him, endured the cross, scorning its shame, and sat down at the right hand of the throne of God. Consider Him who endured such opposition from sinful men, so that you will not grow weary and lose heart."

Take a moment and think about what this passage really says to you. Maybe it's been a long week. Maybe this week has been tougher than most. Are you tired? Could be something in your life's got you down? Like it or not, that's part of the gig here on earth. It really is okay, and you really are okay. But even if your days and your week have been a little challenging, you've got what it takes to see it through. Keep going. Finish strong.

All those saints who went before you and me and all of us - they're watching. Those saints are your very own personal cheering section, having a pep rally just for you. There's no doubt that sometimes life gets bumpy makes you think you're having a bad day or a rough week. I don't mean say this to be smug or condescending but you're not having a bad day. Yeah, of course it seems like it, but when you take a moment to breathe and think, you will realize that you're okay.

Take a moment and go back in your Bible and read the verses in Hebrews 11 – starting about verse 35 - that leads up the "Therefore..." that is the first word in today's Scripture. When you do, you'll see what a bad day can look like. All those saints did everything they did by and through faith, believing totally in God's promises, and a bunch of them ended up poor, destitute, beaten, battered, tortured, maimed, murdered in horrific ways and not one of them ever got to see the fulfillment of so much as one promise from God. But they did it anyway and *never stopped believing.*

You are not having a bad day. Paul tells us they did all of that and endured all of that just so they could one day sit in the stands of Heaven and watch what you're going to do with your faith. Are you going to persevere? You going to hang in there? You ready to keep running the race? Don't forget, Jesus went through much worse than the others in order to ensure that you could have a chance to keep trying. He did it so that you and I "will not grow weary and lose heart."

You're not having a bad day, or a bad week and your life is not in the misery tank like it seems to be. That's just the devil trying to trick you into being mad at God and frustrated. But you? You are a child of God. You are an heir to all that is perfect and holy and wonderful. You are not a quitter. You are here today and you will tap into God's gifts for you and rise up on wings like eagles and, my Friend, today you are going to SOAR!

Never forget that you are loved by the Creator, the one and only God of the entire universe so you tell the enemy what he can do with his "bad day." You persevere. You endure. You run the race. You focus on Jesus and use the faith He gave you as you overcome and achieve. That's your plan for today! "Nothing is impossible for you!" **Matthew 17:20**. Go make it happen!

"This is the day the Lord has made!...." So, what are you going to do with this day? Here's your chance....Now get out there and make this a Power Day.

NOTES

Proverbs 1:5: "...let the wise listen and add to their learning, and let the discerning get guidance..."

"Learn of the skillful. He that teaches himself has a fool for a master." **Benjamin Franklin**

Take a closer look and you may notice something interesting by comparing Benjamin Franklin's 'Learn of the skillful...' to God's 'let the wise listen...'. Did you see it? In order to apply either, or both, of these to one's life, the student is called to pay attention to someone more knowledgeable and experienced. The student doesn't learn on his own.

God's word is also reflected in Mr. Franklin's quote when he mentions the foolishness of being self-taught. "Let the discerning get guidance." If you're like many others, you're probably wanting some proof or example to show the accuracy of the preceding statement. Okay, a real-life example of the wisdom of God as related by Ben Franklin and put into practical reality. In my efforts to complete a college degree, I combined a variety of paths including traditional classroom time with a professor and some correspondence study. I did that because I worked overseas at the time and finding a suitable classroom was somewhat difficult. Fortunately, where I worked, I was able to find a few people who were skilled and helpful on some of the correspondence courses so I had a teacher to help me learn. For the rest, I read the book, went through a lot of paper making endless attempts to understand the material and just as best I could. My experience confirmed, at least, for me, that having a teacher who knows and thoroughly understands the subject matter is vastly superior and more highly advantageous to learning as opposed to going it alone. When you're alone, let's face it, you do a lot of guessing. You have to spend time "reinventing the wheel" so it's slower and more work. Sure, you do the best you can to follow the book but when there's no one to explain all the finer points, the whys and wherefores, and all the tricks and tips the books don't tell you, you're really just hoping for the best. And those guesses are more often wrong. What if the doctor doing your surgery tomorrow was self-taught? Would that give you any concern? Would you like to have carpentry work done in your home by a man who 'read a book somewhere' and is pretty sure this type of nail will work? Think about what you do for a living. You probably have some significant education to your credit...but what you really learned that made you successful were the people who walked you through a lot of hands-on learning. I am the guy who needs to be shown how to do something. I'm visual. If I see it once or twice, I get it. If I can only read about it, it's going to take a while. Learning is a wonderful thing and God thinks very highly of it if Proverbs is any indication. The very best education anyone can have is at the feet...at the side...under the careful and caring eye of someone more experienced and knowledgeable than ourselves. Self-taught is sometimes necessary but usually, it's only good for a little. You can always learn something useful from other people. Everyone else knows something you don't know. *You know something they don't.* You also are a teacher! Give that some thought as you walk through this day.....because.....

"This is the day the Lord has made. Rejoice and be glad in it." Smile - Learn. Teach. Learn more. Teach more. Repeat. Now get out there and make this a Power Day.

Matthew 6: 9 (Amplified Bible): "Pray, therefore, like this: Our Father Who is in heaven, hallowed be Your name."

Read that verse again. Do you see it? It's as plain as the nose on our face and all too often, we just flat miss it. Do you see it? Perhaps one of the most important words in Scripture but certainly in this verse. "Our Father Who _IS_....." "Is..." Our Father....is. He's not going to be. It's not that He _was_. He is not a figment of someone's imagination or a pipedream or the result of wishful thinking. Get this...it's important...."Our Father _IS_."

So maybe you're thinking, "Okay, calm down! We know that...so...?" Answer me this: You know that our Father is....what? While you let that roll around in your head for a moment, give some thought to what the phrase, "Our Father is...," does for your faith. Try these ideas on and see what you think. Our Father is God! Our Father is here. God is what we need. We don't have to wait. We don't have to jump through hoops or click our heels three times and wish really hard.....He is. Already.

Maybe today you're thinking you need something extra special to help you through your day. Here, you have it. Our Father is...your help. Right now. Or, perhaps you're worried about some situation in your life and you are feeling desperate for an answer. Our Father is...the solution. There is the situation in which you have to make a tough but important decision and you are searching for the right direction. Our Father is...the Way.

Are you getting down to your last shelf of stuff? Who's going to provide? Our Father is. Are you afraid you could be in danger from someone or something? Who will protect me? Our Father is. Maybe you're feeling a little helpless and wondering who is going to do this impossible task. Our Father is going to do it. You just believe and watch and learn and grow your faith. And thus the phrase expands to "Our Father, Who is." That's a powerful statement. Does it sound a little hokey and kind of "pie-in-the-sky"-ish? Do you wonder how we can know all this is true? If you think about it, really, the real question is how anyone can not believe the truth of God. Maybe you're one to believe in coincidences. Sorry, but there are no coincidences.

Nothing "just happens." There could be 'God-incidences', maybe but not coincidences. Each time something in your life just "kind of, sort of" worked out for the best....that didn't just happen. Every time you were "*that close*" to abject failure or disgrace or certain demise in some area of your life and you muttered "Dear God!".....and suddenly, "you" found the answer; "you" saved the day; "you" solved the puzzle; "you" turned a bad deal into something great. Uhm, that really wasn't "you"....that was 100% God. Why? Because our Father is. Let me ask a second time: What does it do for your faith to see Our Father in that light? He is the Alpha and Omega. He is the Creator. He is the Way, the Truth, and the Life. He is the Mighty Counselor. He is the Prince of Peace. He is the Lion of Judah. He is the Lamb. He is the Rock, the Shield, the Provider, the Tower of Refuge. Start your day knowing in your heart of hearts, in the very marrow of your soul....Our Father Is...Who? Our Father....Lord, King, God of the whole universe....your Father who loves you. That's Who our Father is.

"This is the day the Lord has made. Rejoice! And be glad in it." Smile - Knowing Who your Father is strengthens your soul. Now get out there and make this a Power Day.

Psalm 95: 1-3 (NIV): "Come, let us sing for joy to the Lord; let us shout aloud to the Rock of our salvation. Let us come before Him with thanksgiving and extol Him with music and song. For the Lord is the great God, the great King above all Gods."

On the off chance that you were wondering what you might do today, tomorrow, or any other day, for that matter....how about taking time to give God your thanks and spend some time praising Him? Even though the Thanksgiving holiday only comes once per year, every day should be a day of, and for, thanksgiving.

Yes, we celebrate and remember how the Pilgrims came to the New World, as it was known at the time. They survived immense and intense hardships, made incredible sacrifices, faced disease and one major challenge after another so they took time to show their gratitude to God for getting them through all of that.

Today, perhaps you can invest some of your time pondering over things you have in your life for which you can be thankful. You have a home, transportation, good health and access to medical care, a family, employment, or a business. All of these are important. Look back to some of the experiences (good, bad or in-between) you've been through and look for the places you can now see where God's hand was working in those situations. Very often events happen in our lives where we must endure this or that and when it's over and we're moving on, we might mumble something that sounds vaguely like "thank God" ...and that's it. Eventually, we put it out of our minds and move on. I'm not saying that's entirely bad but just stop for a moment and look more closely at that circumstance. Hindsight, they say, is 20-20, so maybe, if we look deeper, we'll see something we may have missed before. Do you really know how "that" happened? Maybe you thought it was your friend or mom or Uncle Fred who handled "that" but realized it could only have been God! Now there's something you just "saw again for the first time." Something for which you can now turn to God and sincerely say, "Thank you!"

How many of those types of situations are there in your life? If you're anything like me.....plenty. The "Rock of our salvation" did all that. He _is_ great! And these are the reasons why we can shout His praises, come before Him and worship with song and gladness and thanksgiving. When we take the time to really see God's love and mercy and protection, to focus on His intelligence and the hope He provides, realize where our confidence came from and who lent us the skill and see how it is moving in our lives, then we come to know and understand all He really does for us. I will confidently declare that's worth the effort it takes to give Him His due. The Pilgrims knew that way back when they arrived here. That's why they took the time to celebrate and just be grateful. Never forget that. Always be thankful to God for all He does in our lives. Sing, worship, praise, and say thanks. Celebrate thanksgiving every day and be blessed, happy and know that you are highly appreciated and greatly loved. Thank you for being who you and who you are in Christ.

"This is the day the Lord has made. Rejoice! And be glad in it." Smile - Strive to see God in every step of your walk with Him. Now get out there and make this a Power Day.

Something To Ponder:

"Not what we say about our blessings, but how we use them, is the true measure of our thanksgiving." **W. T. Purkiser**(1)

When we consider the realm of "food for thought," Mr. Purkiser offers us a banquet of potentially life changing options to think about. His quote brings to mind a couple of strong ideas God shares with us in the Book of James.

Recall a time you received a gift. It was a blessing from someone – a friend or a loved one who invested their time, effort, and treasure to find that blessing just for you. You accepted it and returned to the giver a polite smile and a cordial 'thank you.' Not long after that, whatever gift they gave you ends up out of sight, high on the closet shelf, in the back corner, unused, not thought about and unappreciated. Truth be told, you barely gave that thing a second thought. The blessing goes unused and wasted.

Maybe you have given friends and family gift certificates as a gift. Two years later, they still have the certificate. It's never been used. What good is it? Well, of course, any gift that goes unused is full of potential but until it's used, it is no good. How do you, as the giver of that gift, feel knowing your gift to that person was, for all intents and purposes useless, unappreciated, and wasted effort? That the love that went into that had been completely ignored? Hmm.

James 2:18, "But someone will say, 'You have faith, I have deeds.' Show me your faith without deeds, and I will show you my faith *by what I do*." (emphasis mine) Talk all you want....but actions are what I "hear." Action counts. In other words, to paraphrase Mr. Purkiser, the true meaning of thanksgiving *is manifested in what we do* with our blessings...not in how we talk about them. **James,** again, in **Chapter 1,** the last part of **verse 25** (yes, I'm taking it out of context to make a point) "...he will be blessed in what he does." A favorite quote is one I look at often, and I believe it was George B. Shaw who said: "Deeds. Not words." Remember St. Francis of Assisi? He suggested that we "Preach the Gospel very day. If necessary, use words."

All this to make a simple point today. You and I have been continuously and mightily blessed in so many ways by God with gifts we can use to serve Him by serving others. You can see those blessings all around you in every aspect of your life. All I want you to do today is answer this one simple question: Is what you're doing with those blessings demonstrating true thankfulness to God? Today, you are blessed.

"This is the day the Lord has made. Rejoice! And be glad in it." Smile - God gave us all a valuable 'gift certificate.' It would be wise to use it. Now get out there and make this a Power Day.

(1) W.T. Purkiser, AZQuotes.com, Wind and Fly LTD, 2021. https://www.azquotes.com/author/22408-W-T-Purkiser, accessed April 16, 2021.

Psalm 100 (NIV): "Shout for joy to the Lord, all the earth. Worship the Lord with gladness, come before Him with joyful songs. Know that the Lord is God. It is He who made us, and we are His, we are His people, the sheep of His Pasture. Enter His gates with thanksgiving and His courts with praise, give thanks to Him and praise His name. For the Lord is good and His love endures forever; His faithfulness continues through all generations."

We could spend a long and wonderful time talking about all the great and important ideas contained in this Psalm. Today, though, let's focus on two larger pieces of this.

The psalmist begins by addressing the condition of our hearts. Or, more accurately, what condition our hearts should be in. Shout for *joy*...with gladness....singing *joyful* songs. Kindly notice that it does not say anything like; "If your circumstances are perfect and the planets are all lined up and everything in your world is in tip-top shape, then go ahead and be *joyful* and glad." Nor does it speculate about what our circumstances might be, at all. It does not tell us to "be happy," either. Rather, it says be *joyful*. *Joy* and happiness are not the same thing. *Joy* is a heart condition...happiness is an emotional state we choose.

People can be in embroiled in dire circumstances. People can be very unhappy and still be *joyful* in the Lord. *Joy* and gladness spring from growing a close, deep, and meaningful relationship with the Almighty which allows us to find confidence in God based on who and what He is, and who we are *in* Him. *Joy* goes beyond the finite while happiness is circumstantial. For instance, things at work could be in a real mess with people not showing up, work is not getting done or is delayed, others are pulling double duty and deadlines are being missed. The boss is aggravated, everyone is on edge and no one is even a little bit happy. But we can still have joy in the Lord because we know God is in control and no matter what happens, everything will pan out according to God's good will and plan. The more we praise Him, the more we are able to cope, endure, and succeed.

It is joy, then, that helps us see that the Lord is God! We are assured of who God is - the Creator, our Father, and in whom we place all our trust. We are still His People, His flock, still solely dependent on Him and He is faithful to His people. With that joy and confidence and the gladness we gain from it - what then? _Then_ we can be thankful and enter His gates with an attitude of thanksgiving, praising Him. What are His gates and thank Him for what? His gates and His courts are an analogy using a structure like a large room or a courtyard to represent entering into God's presence. We go directly to God, with joy in our hearts, gladness in our minds, to praise Him for all He's done and for who He is....and to just say 'Thank You!'

It's like that all the time, every day because _God is_ all the time, every day. Can you use some good news today to enhance your life? Spend the day, no matter what you're doing or where you are, in the presence of God. Praise Him for everything from the seemingly insignificant to the immense and thank Him for all He has done, is doing, and will do. Every day is a great day to be thankful but especially now as we know that God is always here for us. Do that throughout the day and watch what happens to your life. You'll find yourself being thankful for more than you ever expected.

"This is the day the Lord has made. Rejoice! And be glad in it." Smile - I am thankful for amazing brothers and sisters in Christ. What are you thankful for? Now get out there and make this a Power Day.

NOTES

Revelation 2:3-5: "You have persevered and have endured hardships for my name and have not grown weary. Yet I hold this against you: You have forsaken your first love. Remember the height from which you have fallen! Repent, and do the things you did at first."

In Matthew 6:34, Jesus makes a fact statement that, on its face, might seem to be just a bit weird. He tells us "every day will have trouble of its own." Ever feel like you're walking blindly through a complicated maze and you can hardly take two steps without bumping into another new stumbling block? Day in and day out, you're faced with challenges, setbacks, trials and disappointments. As time went on, you began to grow weary of this experience. Oh, at first, you were strong, and you fought back, determined to persevere. You turned to God for everything no matter how big or small. But, after a while, all those trials, hardships and battering started to hurt. The hurt turned to real pain that manifested in the bruises of faded hope and strained faith that seemed to show up in every area of your life. While you say you are determined to hang in there and you're willing to fight on, underneath the bravado and stoic face, you are very angry, frustrated and feeling lost. Whether or not you want to admit it, the truth is, either by accident or on purpose, you took a wrong turn somewhere and the path you're on now, isn't God's path. You're a bit lost. The one thing that's most important fell off your agenda.

This is sort of what the Ephesians were experiencing in this passage. It happens to almost every new Christian (and even seasoned ones); they start out great. They are standing firm in their beliefs for God and holiness, against heresy and false teachers. Life is good and challenges are mere bumps in the road. But then, somewhere along the line, their motivation wanes, leading to a greater loss of compassion. They grow weary of all the 'stuff' life and the enemy throws at them and begin making bad decisions. They eventually find themselves trying to perseverance through battles that are not even theirs to fight. The battles belong to the Lord. In their wildest imaginations, they couldn't win those battles. None of us can win any battle that is the Lord's to fight. Frustrated, weary, and perhaps feeling hopeless, their love for people gets weak. They forget where they started from and the reasons why they started in the first place.

People. Who created all those people? God. By extension, then, when they stopped loving people, God says they had stopped loving Him. "You have forsaken your first love." (V.4) And we can see how that affected them because we fall into the same trap all the time. We get so bogged down in the struggle and are so determined to fight the good fight...we end up just fighting. We stop loving others as we should. We are forsaking our first love - God.

We can tell when we're there, too. We are overly tired and become irritable. Maybe we find ourselves grumbling about little things. We'll catch ourselves spouting off Scripture without realizing we're using it as a weapon instead of healing help. We're angry at God but won't admit it and yet we hear our own mouth say things like, "I don't know why God won't help me! I'm doing all this for Him! Where is He in all this?!" We all do that from time to time. We all forget "the main thing" and that it still needs to be "the main thing."

Today, if you're tired and frustrated and feel like you're wandering blindly through that maze that is battering you so hard....stop. Stand still. Take a moment to just be quiet. Open your eyes and really take the time to see where you are and what you're doing. Let it sink it. Sshh! Don't say anything...just look. When that sinks in, then repent and remember why you started this journey in the first place. Recall that you really want to do the right and best thing. It's time to come back to ground zero. You need to return to your first love. Love God. In so doing, you can begin to love people again...including yourself. And you will find peace and a way to stop fighting so you can instead, persevere. Just love God first and most.

"This is the day the Lord has made. Rejoice! And be glad in it." Smile - When loving God is first in your mind and heart, you will gain a proper perspective in all things. Now get out there and make this a Power Day.

Romans 8: 15-16 NASB: "For you have not received a spirit of slavery leading to fear again, but you have received a spirit of adoption as sons by which we cry out "Abba! Father!" The Spirit Himself bears witness with our Spirit that we are children of God."

Here's something we all need to not just remember but ponder in our hearts today. You and I are adopted. GOD is our Father.

Let's think for a minute about what it means to be adopted. Having our own children is part of God's plan and it is a wonderful and exciting and holy thing. Indeed, of all the things I've ever done or experienced in my life, being a dad is easily in the top three best experiences for which I'm grateful.

A lot of parents, my wife and I included, can say at least one child came along who was unexpected. Unplanned pregnancy probably happens more often than we realize. However, I'm guessing you've never heard about an unplanned adoption. It's probably extremely rare if it ever happens at all. Adoption is generally only done on purpose. Adoption requires the child to do nothing. The work is all done by the adoptive parents and the adoption agency. They're the ones who plan and handle every detail covering who, what, where, when, and how. The adoptive parents pay all the required costs. Whatever sacrifices are necessary, all of those are made by the parents. They complete any and all work that needs to be accomplished. The child waits until all of that is finished. Think about that.

Children normally are not adopted for the skills they bring to the table. Their God-given attributes are not usually up for consideration. A child gets adopted because a caring, kind someone came along, wanting to simply love them just as they are. It is rare a child is asked to audition for the role of "the new kid." Meeting prospective new parents is decidedly not an audition. It's far more profound, deeper than that. The kids are never charged a fee for this chance. The children should never be told, "You have to do these things in order to earn someone's love, so they'll adopt you." A great many children are adopted when they're still babies so about the only things they can do are look cute, coo, fidget, and be lovable. Older kids who get adopted simply say "yes" if that's their desire. Adoption is deliberate. It's not an impulse. No one simply wakes up one morning and decides to adopt. It's a well-thought out, planned, deliberate act of love designed solely to help make at least one life better.

Why would God do that for us? He already knows everything about each of us and yet, He does it anyway. Why? The answer is in **Ephesians 1:5.** He wanted to. That's it. He loved us and just wanted to. The NIV says, "He predestined us to be adopted as His sons through Jesus Christ, *in accordance with His pleasure and will...*" He adopted us on purpose. Let that sink in. No matter who you are. No matter what you are. Regardless of what you look like, sound like, smell like, how rich or poor, talented or clumsy, whatever you are, AND regardless of what you've ever done - God deliberately took the time, because of His own desire, to love you, to seek you out, and *ask you* for the chance to be your Father. All you have to do is say "yes" and you'll be fully vested into His family and afforded everything blessing given to any child of God Almighty. An abundant life. Mercy. Forgiveness. Grace. Love. Hope. Courage. Healing. Salvation! And best of all - a Father. He does all of this for you because He wants to. Let me ask you today, do you need a Father who loves you? Do you need support that never fails? Do you need someone who accepts you completely? God wants to adopt you. Say, "yes."

"This is the day the Lord has made. Rejoice! And be glad in it." Smile – It's joy knowing you never have to be an orphan. Now get out there and make this a Power Day.

Something to Ponder:

"It is better to be hated for what we are than to be loved for what we are not."
Andre Gide

Hate. It's an emotion of very strong dislike or hostility towards something or someone. What, or who, do you hate? As you think about and begin to visualize that, let me help you focus and be sure you know what it is you're really looking at. Prepare yourself for this because it's a good bet you've probably never looked at this way before. Here it is: _Whatever_ it is (person, place, idea or thing) your hatred of that stems from something rooted inside of you.

Consider this: We humans have no feelings whatsoever about anything that isn't part of us. Let that sink in for a moment. I put it to you that it's impossible to gin up feelings as intense as love or hatred for anyone or anything we don't know. There must be some kind of personal connection. Given that, it's possible for us to love or hate concepts or actions and not hate a person, do you agree? For example, God hates sin but loves you. You love your children but aren't always thrilled with things they do. The point is that you and I are who and what we are. There are people who have a clear understanding of who and what they are, and the rest are still on the path of self-discovery. Either way, no matter who and what we are, there are plenty of people in this world who will hate us because of it. Count on it.

Radical Islamists hate us already. Hence all the attacks on our people around the world in the recent past. Closer to home and even more recent are groups like Antifa and BLM who absolutely despise us. They don't hate us as individuals. Rather, they hate what _they think_ we represent. They hate us for what we are. If you converted to Islam, or became a socialist, or renounced your current beliefs, the very same people who now hate you would suddenly love who and what you are. "You" is the concept...not you personally. The question then becomes: are you willing to be hated for what you are? You're a Christian. You made a voluntary, willful choice to live according to the ideals, teachings, and commands of God Almighty. A lot of people around the world and in your own country hate you for that based on what _they think_ a Christian is – which may or may not be accurate. As silly as that is, it's a fact but it allows for a very clear idea of just how much power that concept possesses. Even more sobering is the fact that those same people who hate you for being Christian are willing to kill or be killed over our differing ideas of who God is. Are you? Willing, that is. Would you give your life for your God, for your beliefs? Many have and do so daily. All the disciples were willing and only one was not martyred. Jesus was not only willing, it was part of the Father's plan to begin with. Jesus jumped at the opportunity, ("..for the joy set before Him" **Heb. 12:2**) except He surprised a lot of folks and came back. If He hadn't, this book you're reading never would have existed.

Powerful stuff: being hated and being willing to be hated for who and what you are. It takes guts to do that. The other option is living the deception of being loved for who you are not. Those who "love" the ones living the lie are actually quite selfish. They don't love *you* but rather love only who or what they want you to be. A lot of people live a lie because they mistakenly think that's the only way others will like, love or accept them. Those who live that way often end up hating themselves and that's far worse. There are a lot of homeless, destitute people on the streets who are highly educated and very smart, but they tried being something they weren't, and it brought them down. Lies always do that eventually. _We cannot be who we are not_ and make it work for very long, even if others love us for it.

The solution is to "know the truth and the truth will set you free!"(**John 8:32**) Your life is *YOUR* life! Live it being who you really are and accept that there are others who see something inside themselves that will cause them to hate you. But there will be far more who will love you for who are and see right through who you are not. God went to a lot of trouble to make YOU. Be that person.

"This is the day the Lord has made. Rejoice! And be glad in it." Smile - Invest yourself in who God made you to be. That's living! Now get out there and make this a Power Day.

Deuteronomy 2: 24-25: "Set out now and cross the Arnon Gorge. See, I have given into your hands Sihon the Amorite, king of Heshbon, and his country. Begin to take possession of it and engage him in battle. This very day I will begin to put the terror and fear of you on all the nations under heaven. They will hear reports of you and will tremble and be in anguish because of you."

The nation of Israel was still wandering around in the desert. They had not yet gone into the Promised Land. The time had come for them to _start_ receiving what God has provided for them. Notice that in this case, they couldn't simply receive it...they had to take it. "...engage him in battle" is what God said.

God had done some preparation work on behalf of Israel. He made it possible for them to succeed but they are the ones charged with actually carrying it out. Sound familiar? God gives us tools and gifts to use but for those tools and gifts to be effective, we must _use_ them. God even went so far as to give the Israelites the kind of reputation that struck fear in the hearts of "all the nations under heaven." Everyone was afraid of the Israelites. They were, according to their God-given reputation, an unbeatable army. In those days, it was widely believed that a military victory was possible only with divine help. The god of the conquering nation was superior to the god of the defeated nation. Here, that was very true and always is with God since no god (little g) will ever defeat the one, true God (Capital G). The army with all the wins was the army whose God was superior to all.

God tells His people to "_begin_" doing what He had told them to do. In essence, "_Go_ where I tell you to go. _Take_ what I've prepared for you." God gives them a pep talk; "I did all the PR work. I got the minds and hearts of the opposition where they need to be. They won't resist too much....Go get 'em." Moses had first sent a message to Sihon. He was trying to be the nice guy and ask permission from Sihon to cross Heshbon. Moses even offered to buy food and water. Sihon not only refuses, but he sends his army to stand in their way. So, God's response sounds like, "Okay, Moses, you were polite and this dude's just won't play by the rules and he's used up all his chances. Take him out and move on." Sihon's army and family get wiped out.

Cool story with all the makings of a great mini-series on the Gospel Movie Channel. But how does it apply to you and me today? We have a purpose which God has given us to fulfill and He's telling us...."I've given 'Today' into your hands. I've made all the preparations. I've made it possible for you to succeed. Everything you need to succeed is in place. Now, you begin... you start...you go....you take..." A major part of the success of any endeavor is simply to begin, to go, to take what God says is yours. It is true that once you begin a worthwhile endeavor, all manner of support appears seemingly out of the woodwork to assist you with that. What makes today the perfect day to begin that is God has already laid the groundwork for your success. He's the Father, standing in the shallow end of the pool with His arms stretched out to catch you and He's saying, "Come on, Kid! Jump in!"

You have a choice. If you want to swim and enjoy all the benefits of being in the pool, you must begin. Jump in. Go to the arms of the Father. You have to take all He has for you. Do that, and the Promised Land is yours. Or, you can sit on the edge of the pool - looking in, wishing and wondering. It's a new day...God set you up to experience victory. Go get it!

"This is the day the Lord has made. Rejoice! And be glad in it." Smile - God already did His part. We must do ours. Now get out there and make this a Power Day.

2 Cor. 8:11: "Now finish the work, so that your eager willingness to do it may be matched by your completion of it, according to your means."

The deadline is drawing close. The project due date is just over the horizon, and you have three, maybe four days counting today, depending on your work schedule to finish your work for this project. Maybe some tweaking can spill over beyond the deadline, but the main thrust of this task must be completed now. You know how it is when the end of a task is that close. You feel rushed and like the work is dragging at the same time. Chances are you're tired and maybe a bit frustrated. Scripture says we should complete the work in a manner that matches our *"eager willingness to do it....according to our means."*

What does that mean? Allow me to offer my take on this and you decide if you agree. I will claim there are three ways for work to be completed. Two of them aren't so hot. Often, people start out on a project filled with excitement and enthusiasm. But as time goes by and they get close to the end, the work has exacted a toll and they can be tired. It's been a long haul and no matter how well planned this project was, there are always challenges and unexpected trials to deal with and they're worn out. Even though they can see the end in sight, they lose heart. The energy to push the last few inches to the goal line fades and they just stop trying. Or, take the same basic scenario but instead of quitting, they opt to do "whatever" just to finish this thing and be done with it. Probably not their best work. Maybe they substituted in one area with inferior materials. The work isn't up to par, but who cares! It's done. They spent a massive amount of time on this project, put forth all that effort, dealt with all the stuff that came with it, and at the end, they ease up and stop with something beneath their best efforts. They finish...but not strong. They finish weak simply because they just want to be done with it. Have you ever been there?

Let me ask you - What if God, who "began a good work in you and is faithful to complete it" decided that completing you was a "whatever" situation? What do you think our lives would be like if He just got bored or tired of completing His work in us? The good news is that's not how God works. It is good for us to follow His example and not finish weak, either. Finally, the third option. There are those to whom this Scripture is really talking. Those who started strong and who are bound and determined to finish at least that strongly if not more so. They have a commitment to excellence. They want to give their very best all the way to the end and won't settle for anything less. That's how one matches their eager willingness to do a work with the completion of it. And they finish it with the resources they have. They don't waste time fretting over what they don't have. Instead, they combine what they have with their willingness to use it properly because that's how it will be accepted. The very next verse (12) says, *"For if the willingness is there, the gift is acceptable according to what one has, not according to what he does not have."* Your willingness to excel, using what you have to work with, striving to do the best you can and finish strong is what gains acceptance. Today, finish strong. Don't fret over what you don't have but apply your best efforts using what you do have and finish your work with the same level of excitement and enthusiasm you had when you began. And remember to give God the glory.

"This is the day the Lord has made. Rejoice and be glad in it." Smile - Invest your best time and effort and reap a good harvest. Now get out there and make this a Power Day.

NOTES

Something To Ponder:

Shortest, Most Effective Lesson on Selling: (1) Know their business. (2) Know your stuff. **Source Unknown.**

High pressure sales tactics are truly annoying and generally make potential buyers walk away or endure a lousy buying experience. If you're anything like me, you are not a fan of such sales tactics. Give me someone who is ready and willing to help me solve my problem by steering me to what I actually need and want. But there are those salespeople whose goal is to brow beat us into a sale.

I will venture a guess you've run into high pressure salespeople more than once in your life. If you've been to a car lot or a furniture store, chances are good. What is high pressure? It's a sales tactic designed to press you into submission and to buy whatever they're selling just to get them off your back. They won't take no for an answer unless and until you all but force them to stop trying. Rarely in their sales pitches or their readymade "objection deflectors" will they ask what it is you really need. Any effort to get to know anything about you is blatantly fake. Thus, they have no understanding of your situation or what you need to solve a problem. It's all about them, their products or service, and why you should buy only from them. Right now! Wow! That's exhausting.

The most effective salespeople seem to know more about the potential client's business or their customers before they ever enter the office or a store's sales floor. They ask relevant questions without being pushy. These salespeople listen to answers and take the time to find the right solution for the need. Ironically, the only time they talk about product or service is to answer questions. Otherwise, their focus is on the client or customer, the business and its needs and goals. It's relational. When the time is right to "close the deal" they present two or three options which would serve the purpose and truly meet the needs and desires of the customer. A relationship based on trust is built. Friendship ensues. Friends buy from friends. High pressure leaves you frustrated and feeling used. A truly good salesperson doesn't sell you anything. He helps you solve a problem by giving you solutions that work based on what you told him you needed. Face it, if you wanted to buy a new sofa for $ 600 or less in a particular color and style, you'll most likely buy from someone who shows you options that match what you wanted. The right price, the right color, the right style, and you can have it now. Sign here. Done. You're happy - you got what you wanted. He's happy, he made a sale and earned a living and now has a repeat customer because he knew your business and he knew his stuff. Okay. Nice tale but what does that have to do with you and your Christian walk today?

God created you to be one-of-a-kind. There is not one other human on the face of this earth exactly like you. You have a skill set that is totally unique and you need to know what that is. You need to fully understand who and what you are because your skills are the solution to a problem someone else has. Knowing your stuff will lead you to find what business of "theirs" you should know. No force or high pressure will be needed because your skills and knowledge will build a relationship which leads to a solution, which leads to a longer-term relationship, which will allow you the opportunity to speak into the life of others about the love of God. And that's your primary calling, isn't it? Know your stuff so you can know them so you can share the Good News.

"This is the day the Lord has made. Rejoice! And be glad in it." Smile - "It's not just a job...." Relationship is solution. Now get out there and make this a Power Day.

Matthew 1:22-23: "All this took place to fulfill what the Lord had said through the prophet: 'The virgin will be with child and will give birth to a son, and they will call Him Immanuel' - which means, "God with us.""

It is most common to see this verse and others like it only around Christmas time. However, I am going to suggest such a verse is good to remember all the time. Why? Because it's hard to think of any day when His name, Immanuel, "God with us" would not apply. Name a day God isn't with us. Yeah, I can't either.

There are questions that come with this verse. First, looking at the first line might prompt you to wonder, all *what* took place? Secondly, which prophet did God speak through about the virgin being with child? With a little digging, we find the answer to the second question is Isaiah. Look in that Old Testament book's 7th chapter and 14th verse and see how Matthew is quoting Isaiah word for word. That prophesy was made 900 years *before* the birth. So, "all this..." started with everything that happened from the time Isaiah made the prophecy and built up to the day Mary got a visit from the Angel of the Lord.

The answer to the first question is a bit more involved. See, Mary and Joseph were betrothed. In those days - as it should be today – betrothal was a very big deal. It was as if they were already married but just didn't have the paperwork yet. So, when Matthew says, "Mary was found to be with child," it is before the official wedding has taken place. Mary is technically still single but spoken for and Joe was, shall we say, less than thrilled.

He had to be thinking the same sorts of things you and I would think. "Mary is a virgin but she's pregnant. And the Holy Spirit is taking credit for it! What the....?! I'm going ...she's going to be...we're both going to be....oh man, we are in deep trouble! Mary's going to be disgraced! What am I supposed to do? She's got a kid that isn't mine! They could stone her to death for that! Marrying Mary won't be too merry. I'll divorce her. That's it! I'll divorce her - quietly - so no one knows and we'll send her somewhere...and...." Joseph was really struggling with this situation. Being who He is, God didn't let Joe struggle too long and sent an angel to talk to him. "Joseph, son of David, do not be afraid to take Mary home as your wife...." and the angel went on to clue Joseph to what was happening. "Ohhhh! Now I get it. Well, in that case...sure, of course."

Think about Joseph's mind set and heart for a moment. Think about Mary's, too. Here are two everyday folks, doing their best to get along. They're in love and looking forward to a great wedding day. One night, the craziest dream shows up in Mary's head. "Yo, Mary, God here....got this crazy idea....you can help. C'mon, you want to? You get to be the *Mother of God*! I know, that's a little bit – well, a lot shocking but hey, trust me. How 'bout it, Kid, ya wanna help?" "Hey, Joseph, Buddy, Pal....Dude, check it out....your wife to be... sweet girl and so caring...man, she's like, you know...pregnant but hey...she's still virgin. Don't let that throw you, though, Joe, 'cause the baby is really... seriously...God's son. Just like Isaiah told your people hundreds of years ago. Dude, this prophesy is like coming true! And you get to be sort of a step-dad to the Son of God Almighty....K?"

Tell me if that happened to you, you'd be thinking, "Oh, okay." No, you wouldn't. You'd be stressed, overwhelmed, scared, excited and you'd run the full range of emotions and spiritual feelings. All of that and a lot more had to happen in order to fulfill the prophesy. It took 900 years to see Jesus coming to us. Coming to Jesus is, likewise, really not so easy or quick, is it? It takes time. It's a process and much more than "All you have do is" pray the sinner's prayer and you're done. That's only part of it. What does it take to get someone to a point in their life where they sincerely pray that prayer? That's why it's so important for us to tell people what Christmas, and every day is really all about. Immanuel, God with us. Tell 'em why.

"This is the day the Lord has made. Rejoice! And be glad in it." Smile - Now get out there and make this a Power Day.

Psalm 73: 3-5 and 17: "For I envied the arrogant when I saw the prosperity of the wicked. They have no struggles; their bodies are healthy and strong. They are free from the burdens common to man; they are not plagued by human ills. ....till I entered the sanctuary of God; then I understood their final destiny."

If you've been Christian for any reasonable amount of time, chances are you've joined fellow believers in walking through the spiritual battle in which you suffered and struggled with life's issues while non-believers seemed to prosper in every area of their lives. You know the situation. So-n-So cheats on his wife, is a real hardcase at work, and has no idea what "Generosity" truly means. And forget ever thinking that guy will forgive anyone of anything but he's doing great in his business. Despite his skill in bad behavior, he's got all the "right" friends, he's wealthy and life for him seems amazing.

In the meantime, you focus on playing by the rules. You do your best to work hard and remain loyal to your spouse and kids. You strive to walk upright consistently with prayer, worship, you give above and beyond. You always make time for reading the Word and....and it seems like you couldn't catch a break if jumped into your arms. That's more than just a little disconcerting. You wouldn't be the first or only Believer asking, "Why him and not me? Where is God in all this? How come I suffer for doing it right and he's getting all sorts of goodies for doing it wrong?"

That's the exact same territory where the psalmist was doing spiritual battle. We've struggled with it before and may be fighting that battle right now. It's a sure bet we will likely struggle with it again at some future point. It causes us to question our faith and how valid is faith really? You recognize the battlefield when you hear yourself asking, "Why bother? Why should I even try?" Well, the psalmist provides mercifully answers those questions.

Look how the psalmist comes around. He realizes he's been looking at others and all this whole situation through human eyes and from a worldly perspective. When he began to draw closer to God ("till I entered the sanctuary of God…") he began to see things more from a spiritual perspective. His whole attitude changed to something more mature and confident. He came to understand some very important ideas. Such as: from the worldly side of things, life isn't fair and it's hard, but the worldly rewards are temporary. Looking through a spiritual lens, with God's help, he could focus on what was truly important and lasting. Namely, our eternal rewards. Eternal rewards are infinitely better than anything the world has to offer.

Today, if that's you and you're wondering why them and not me - if you're thinking, why you should even bother, try adjusting your sights to God's point of view. What is really important? What really matters? Which rewards endure forever, and which fade all too quickly? It has been said that "If you want to change your life....change your mind." Give it a shot. You will be pleasantly surprised.

"This is the day the Lord has made. Rejoice! And be glad in it." Smile - Don't waste too much time worrying about life's fairness and focus more on what is right and what God has for you. Now get out there and make this a Power Day.

Proverbs 29:18 "Where there is no vision, the people perish."

Our dreams, ideas, and the visions God gives us are vital to our lives. We've all had dreams and visions but what grabs our attention are those moments when an idea pops into our head and we wonder, "Where did that come from?" When you experienced that, did you automatically dismiss that idea, or did you invest some time to ponder it? Think about this for a moment because it's important. Way too often, we dismiss truly great ideas that we don't recognize as great because when they come to mind, they just seem silly. In fact, they are something we should cherish because they are the foundation for a remarkable future achievement.

Imagine if the first guy who ever looked at a cow and thought, "I don't know why but it seems like it would be good to squeeze those hangy-downy things and drink whatever comes out of it. Nah. That's just weird." As odd as that sounds, aren't you glad we have milk to drink and cook with? What if Eli Whitney dismissed as "crazy" the idea he had for the cotton gin – a machine that revolutionized the cotton industry? What if Mr. Smith and Mr. Wesson decided that their ideas for handguns were just too radical? This nation would be far different if people like our Founding Fathers, George Washington, Martin Luther King and son, and Abe Lincoln didn't have a vision for our nation that they were willing to explore and bring into reality. Our ideas matter. Your dreams are important.

Granted, when we engage in clear, rational thinking and take all factors into account, we must admit not every idea is from God and we should be a bit selective on which ones we pursue. We do need to exercise some wisdom, judgment, and common sense. By the same token, not every idea that seems silly at the time should be ignored, either. One day, someone had a silly idea and twisted a small piece of wire into a funny shape and presto....paperclips were born. Years ago, some guy figured out it would be great to combine cola syrup with carbonated water in the same container and voila! Bottles of soda pop came to be and revolutionized an industry. As a result of vision and ideas, man really has walked on the moon. Oil, air travel, telephones, textiles, farming, computers and on and on! All of it began with an idea....a vision....a dream.

Here's the kicker: God gives us a lot of great ideas and if we know anything about God at all, we know that sometimes, His ideas may strike us as being a bit "off" at first. Our initial reaction may sound something like, "Seriously? You're kidding, right?" God's ideas sound like: To be first, be last. If you want to be a great leader, be an amazing servant. To really live, die to yourself. Love your enemies. Forgive...especially when the pain hurts most. So, when you get an idea that comes seemingly out of nowhere and it's strange, even for you, you might want to take a little time and mull it over. It could change your life and many lives and then you'd have one more great reason to give God your praise and gratitude and thanks. So, today, what's on your mind?

"This is the day the Lord has made. Rejoice! And be glad in it." Smile - One day God had an idea to save a whole world....with a baby! Your idea could be worth looking into. Now get out there and make this a Power Day.

1 Timothy 2: 5: "For there is one God and one mediator between God and men, the man Christ Jesus..."

In case you had any doubts or were wondering at all, this is one verse of many that might help clear up the question, 'was Jesus really human?" Yes, He was. It is one of life's great mysteries that Jesus was both fully God and fully human at the same time.

If you happen to be, as am I, a fan of history and apologetics, then you might know that in the latter part of the first century, some people bought into a particular heresy known as "Docetism." Docetism comes from the Greek *dokein* meaning "to seem." The people who adhered to this belief claimed Jesus' human body was a phantasm...a vision. He just "seemed" human. Their assertion was that if Jesus was God, He couldn't have suffered on the cross and if He suffered, He couldn't be God. Therefore, it just "looked like" He suffered.

Still today, there are those who question the humanity of Christ, as well. Let's be fair and agree, it is a hard concept to wrap our heads around. He's God. He is man. No, wait! He's both at the same time. However, for those who dare to look at and strive to understand all the evidence, there's no other choice but to accept and believe it. Yes, Jesus was supernaturally conceived. But we must realize his mother was human. Jesus has a human lineage. He was flesh and blood with human characteristics such as being able to experience pain. He had a sense of humor and the entire gamut of emotions just as you and I do. He experienced a horrible, tragic human death. You can find a ton of Scriptural support in Matthew, Luke, John, Romans, 1 Corinthians, Galatians, and more. The amount of historical and archaeological evidence for Jesus is overwhelming.

Okay. Christians have known and understood this for thousands of years so what's the big deal? The big deal is that, especially around the Christmas time of year, many people are still skeptical and make off-the-wall, outrageous claims about God and Jesus. Those who don't know Christ may readily believe or accept such claims without question and those who do know better should be able to explain the truth.

What do you say when someone asks why you celebrate Christmas, claiming it's really just about whatever their favorite misconception happens to be? Perhaps you've heard of Fideism. Maybe not. The idea behind Fideism is that faith cannot possibly be explained by reason. It claims there is no correlation between faith and reason and that God is only faith, so reason has no place in our religion. Before you give credence to that idea, consider that in **Isaiah 1:18**, God says, "Come, let us reason together..." and we're to "love the Lord your God with all your heart, all your soul, and all your *mind*...." as Jesus tells us in **Matthew 22**. Your mind, too, huh? Kind of puts a dent in fideism, doesn't it? Today and every day, there are a lot of people who very much need God and are seeking but they're skeptical or asking questions or are hesitant for some reason. What will you tell them? If you're not sure, there's something you can do today. The Bible says, "Always be prepared to give an answer for the hope you have...." **1 Peter 3:15** You need to know how to answer. Find out.

"This is the day the Lord has made. Rejoice! And be glad in it." Smile - There's a reason God wants us to be knowledgeable and wise. Now get out there and make this a Power Day.

NOTES

Titus 1: 6-9: "An elder must be blameless, the husband of but one wife, a man whose children believe and are not open to the charge of being wild and disobedient. Since an overseer is entrusted with God's work, he must be blameless - not overbearing, not quick-tempered, not given to drunkenness, not violent, not pursuing dishonest gain. Rather he must be hospitable, one who loves what is good, who is self-controlled, upright, holy, and disciplined. He must hold firmly to the trustworthy message as it has been taught, so that he can encourage others by sound doctrine and refute those who oppose it."

Paul says, "an elder ***must be***...." all these things. It makes sense that all elders should be all these things and for good reason. Elders are leaders. An important part of their role is to set an example within the church and their communities for others to follow and it always a good idea that their example reflects God in a positive and constructive manner. Who are the people you think of when you hear the word elder? Most people will automatically imagine a group of men in their church. Yes, some churches have female elders but in the context of Scripture, which is the Word of God, an elder is a man so let's go with that.

I will propose a bit of a challenge for you to wrap your mind around. First, know that an elder or an overseer can be a dad, a husband, a big brother, a guardian, a boss, or frankly, any role that carries some authority with it. You are, for example, an elder in your home. Ergo, my Friend, Paul was talking directly to all of us men which means God's word here definitely applies directly to you and me.

Here's the challenge, Men: Read through this passage again and insert your name where it's appropriate. For instance, "John must be blameless - John's children should believe - John is entrusted with God's work..." and so on. Do that with your name and then read it again. There's a good list of functions and character traits that we're required to practice and become and grow into. Note the word *'required'* because Paul repeatedly used the words "must be." God did not make this list optional. He wasn't suggesting we try to be, or try to do, this: - it's a command. We *must* do this. We *must* be that. Why? In order that we *can* set a good example, lead effectively and know well how to defend our faith with wisdom, love, passion, compassion, honor and strength.

If you haven't already started, there's nothing stopping you from beginning right now to work on this job description and become the man God desires you to be. The benefits are very cool. Your wife will find you highly attractive. Not because you're "all that" but because God in you is irresistible. Your children will not only respect you more, but they will also want to honor you with their obedience. That's not a bad thing. Absolutely, it's a challenge. To be sure, it isn't always easy. Without a doubt, you have to work on it daily and there will be setbacks. Fear not, it's okay. Do it anyway because it's very much worth the effort. Indeed, consider the devastating results of the alternative.

"This is the day the Lord has made. Rejoice! And be glad in it." Smile - A man of God is something we become...it takes time. That's okay. Your job is to take the time. Now get out there and make this a Power Day.

Heb. 11:1 "Faith is being sure of what we hope for and certain of what we do not see."

We can get happy and excited just anticipating what we know will happen "someday." If we know something will happen or we will receive something, we can be happy and excited now. The idea is that while so far, nothing has yet come or happened, something is already here. Here's an illustration: Tell your young child that he or she *will be* getting something they asked for - something they really, really wanted. Notice - they don't have it, yet. All they have so far is your word, your promise, and yet, the joy and sense of hope fulfilled comes pouring out of them. It hasn't manifested yet, but something is already bubbling up inside you. That's what the Scripture is saying. Faith is hope. We know a *good* thing is coming and that gives us a sense of certainty and hope.

Maybe you can recall when you just found out the mortgage was approved or getting that special phone call telling you the job is yours, or hearing, "Honey, it's not just the two of us anymore!" Even though you don't have the house yet, or you've not actually started the new job and it's going to be months before the baby arrives....you know inside what that type of news does for your spirit. Nothing has happened yet but you are already joyful.

You know that one day you will go to your real home, in heaven, and experience everlasting life absent of pain, sickness and despair. There will be nothing whatsoever to cry about and all your mistakes of this world are forgiven and forgotten! Wow! That is a gift you *HAVE NOW* but won't actually experience for a long while. Nothing has happened physically yet, but something very special is already here.

Each day brings something we can celebrate because of Christ. In our hearts and minds, we're already there. That's faith. As the song says, we "don't have to see it to believe it." We know in our bones it's coming. The actual gift or event or person or time or *something* has not yet come but something is already here because there is great joy. We understand hope. We have a vision of a totally different tomorrow and we can see it with a confidence that can only come from God. "Faith is the substance of things hoped for and the evidence of things not seen." Today....you should have some of that. If you don't, get you some. Ask God to help you. Pray for God to show you how to exercise your faith and walk in His way. That's a prayer God will answer. And then you have a really good day.

"This is the day the Lord has made. Rejoice and be glad in it." Smile - Faith moves mountains. Faith heals. Faith restores. Faith liberates your soul. Expect good things! Now get out there and make this a Power Day.

Matthew 25: 40 and 45: "The King will reply, 'I tell you the truth, whatever you did for one of the least of these brothers of mine, you did for me.' "He will reply, 'I tell you the truth, whatever you did not do for one of the least of these, you did not do for me.'"

It may be more pronounced around Thanksgiving and Christmas because those seasons focus much more on giving, selflessness, and gratitude, but this is something we should be mindful of always. How do you decide who to help and who not to extend a hand to? It's a tough call and God applies some pressure by saying when we help the less fortunate or the sick or prisoners, we serve Him and if we don't help, He takes it very personally. What to do?

It is safe to say that, *as individuals*, we probably don't have the means to help every single person or cause that comes along. Although we truly wish we could help more, most of us have to fall back on doing what we can, where we can, when we can. Notice, though, that God never told us in this Scripture to go broke, naked, or homeless and sacrifice everything so we could help everybody. That's a very noble idea but I'm pretty sure God doesn't want you to put yourself or your family in jeopardy do help out, although a true gift does require some amount of sacrifice. Jesus was talking about the condition of our heart and our attitude. The point being we do what we can with a joyful and willing heart for those needing our help. When we see someone in a situation and know can help, and it's clearly the right thing to do, then by all means, joyfully and willingly rush to make the sacrifice and do all you can to help.

The trouble is found in deliberately not helping. We need to understand that it's one thing to not help because we simply don't have the means, or because it would be clearly wrong for a legitimate reason. It's another thing altogether to withhold help because it might be inconvenient or helping would mean "I can't do what I want." If our refusal to help is based on selfishness or laziness or because we just don't care, then Friend, you must know God has a zero-tolerance policy with that. Look at verse 46. "Then they will go away to eternal punishment." Yikes! In other words, not helping when you can help is not an option, ever.

In real life, in your every day, what can you do to help "the least of these"? It could be any of a wide array of different services. Perhaps you could give some personal time to do hospital visits. You could help a neighbor with something. You can always be a "Secret Santa" and ensure the kid whose family is struggling gets a toy for their birthday or that groceries "magically" appear on their doorstep. Any one of a million different things we can do to demonstrate God's love to others can be done by anybody. Why not you? It's helps those who should not be enabled by not enabling them. "Tough love" is a gift of help. It's dying to yourself enough to give cash to someone who needs it more than you when you'd really rather spend that money on something else. It's seeing a table full of troops or police officers at a restaurant and anonymously picking up their tab. It's standing up for someone who's being attacked or harassed. It's being willing to get involved when others are too frightened to speak up. It's *never tying any strings to the gifts you give* or the sacrifices you make and *never expecting nor asking for anything in return* for what you do.

Today, and every day, remember that every person you see is both God's creation and someone Jesus died for and they are worthy of your help. Whatever you do for them, you do for God.

"This is the day the Lord has made. Rejoice! And be glad in it." Smile - Jesus died for us. All He wants us to do is be kind and generous. Good trade! Now get out there and make this a Power Day.

Consider This:

"When it's hard to think of something to write about, I remind myself that compared to what can be known and talked about, the sum of everything that has ever been written, by every writer since time began, is a tiny drop in the ocean of knowledge." **Jeffrey Hill**

Did you know that in today's world, the amount of new information produced every day is 2.5 quintillion bits? That's 1,000 TRILLION or 1 million billion bits of data. Every day. Every *minute* of every day over 4.1 million people watch a YouTube video. Every *second* of every *minute*, 5 new profiles are created on Facebook. Hundreds of millions of emails are sent every minute. The stats are incredible! There is always something new to know. There is an endless supply of topics to talk about. There are more new ideas every hour than all of mankind can address in a typical lifetime. And because there's always someone who hasn't heard and needs to hear it, much of this information has to be repeated. That's a lot of info!

There are two phrases people say that I find highly irritating. One is when anyone says, 'I don't know.' It would be better to say, "I don't know, yet." To me, the person saying they don't know missed a lot because they either took a whole lot for granted, or they don't care, or they're willfully ignorant. We can understand not caring about some things. It's not reasonable to assume everyone cares about everything. It's easy to see how anyone takes certain things for granted. But it's hard to come up with a good excuse for willful ignorance. In this day and age, most of us can find out pretty much anything we want or need to know quickly. If you have a cell phone and access to the internet, the world is at your fingertips. Want to put some excitement in your life every day? It's so very easy to learn something you didn't know before.

The other phrase that just grates on me like fingernails on a chalkboard is "I'm bored." It didn't take much for our kids to learn never to utter those two words in our house because in short order, they would have plenty to do. If we parents had to come up with things for them to do, they probably didn't enjoy it as much as something they might have come up with on their own. All they had to do was try. There is always...always...something to do and something new to learn. Mind you, I don't mean being busy for the sake of being busy. I mean there are things to do that are meaningful, serve a purpose and accomplish something worthwhile. The question, "What did you do today?" should always have an interesting answer that takes the responder a while to talk about. "Not much...." or "Nuthin'" are sad answers indicating someone's life is somehow unfulfilled and in need of a shakeup. Friend, if the shoe fits, wear it!

Okay. Two things: there is always something new to learn and there is always something worthy to do. Always. Witness: When I started writing this devotion, I had no idea what to write about and PRESTO! Writing about *that* turned into something worth remembering. Funny how God does that stuff, huh? So - it's Today. You've got all day! What are you going to do with it?

"This is the day the Lord has made. Rejoice and be glad in it." Smile - In order to live the abundant life Jesus offers, we have to go, and grow, and do. Now get out there and this a Power Day.

Hebrews 12: 1-3: "Therefore, since we are surrounded by such a great cloud of witnesses, let us throw off everything that hinders and the sin that so easily entangles, and let us run with perseverance the race marked out for us. Let us fix our eyes on Jesus, the author and perfector of our faith, who for the joy set before Him endured the cross, scorning its shame, and sat down at the right hand of the throne of God. Consider Him who endured such opposition from sinful men, so that you will not grow weary and lose heart."

Eli was a solder. He was one of the soldiers prayed for on daily by a church group back home. Eli and his unit were stationed in Afghanistan, fighting a war against evil. Eli and his unit were not just fighting who. They were fighting what.

They did battle to stop an enemy bent on the destruction of freedom. That was the "who." They also battled the spirits of gloom, doom, depression, discomfort, loneliness, fatigue, and stress. That was the "what." They endured their own crosses for the joy set before them. What joy? As Eli put it, he was accomplishing "the job I was sent here to do." As Eli and his comrades ran the race marked out for them, they had to throw off everything that hinders. They had to focus. If they didn't, it would have cost lives.

War constantly provides tough circumstances thus it was a rare thing for Eli or his comrades to get something as simple but great as a shower. More often than they would wipe themselves off once a week with baby wipes. Forget having the luxury of a comfy bed to sleep in and you can bet he, and his fellow soldiers got pretty burnt out on MRE's (meals ready to eat) or manna, if you will. It's a dirty, tough, nasty job being a soldier whose mission is to find and engage the enemy head-on.

Unless you're a combat vet, we can only imagine all the other trials Eli and all the troops had to go through while we at home remained comfy and cozy. He got shot at and his life was at risk all day, every day. Some of the men in his unit, his friends, returned home in coffins. Prayers included asking God for Eli's safe homecoming. His tour was extended so he stayed there longer. Enduring. Scorning the shame. Persevering. Fighting the good fight. Not quitting because a job had to be done. A worthy job. A job that was necessary. God blessed Eli and all those who served likewise for what they had to endure, their commanders and all who made it possible for them to have a chance at success.

War is the worst of trials and Jesus is no stranger to such battles. Jesus went into the devil's lair to fight and win necessary battles so we could all one day live free in Heaven. Eli and all our troops inspire me, and I hope they inspire you. They deserve so much more than what I can give by myself, but I can give them my respect. I can honor them. Our military live and serve daily for the cause of freedom much the same as what God is calling all of us to do daily for the cause of freedom in Christ. Today, let me ask you, are you in this fight? Are you enduring? Throwing off all that hinders and persevering? Running your race to the very best of your ability? If so, thank you. For Eli and all those who serve our nation in battle and in support positions wherever you are, God protect and encourage you and keep you safe and successful. Thank you. Today, run your race. Race to win.

"This is the day the Lord has made. Rejoice and be glad in it." Smile -Every day, begin with "on your mark...get set....GO!" Run your race. Now get out there and Make this a Power Day.

NOTES

Matthew 24:44: "So you also must be ready, because the Son of Man will come at an hour when you do not expect Him."

In our culture, when someone says they're coming back, that normally comes with a date, a time and possibly, a place. In our culture, we set appointments, make dates, schedule meetings. Why? We know what to do, where to be, and what will be happening at that time, on that date. We answer the question, "When can we expect you?" before the event ever takes place. We know in advance what to expect. Jesus doesn't play like that. He never answered that question. He simply told us to "…keep watch, because you do not know on what day your Lord will come." **(Verse 42)**.

That bit of biblical truth never stopped some in our nation's history from boldly proclaiming and prophesying the date and time Jesus would return. Whatever "proof" they claimed to have only proved them wrong. How do I know? The Bible is very specific about what will be occurring and all that must happen before Jesus returns. While it is now, and has been for a very long time, a work in progress, not every condition has been met, yet. Some things still need to be completed. Still, we must be ready and stay ready. What does that mean?

When you are anticipating a major presentation for a client at work, or the "big game" or something that is very important to you – do you wait until someone calls you and says, "It's time. Go now!" before you try to prepare? Of course not. Why not? Because if you wait like that, there's no way you can be properly prepared and you'll lose the client, lose the game, or miss that big opportunity. It won't go well for you if you are not prepared. It never does. The only good thing that comes from that scenario is a powerful lesson in humility. To the contrary, you begin preparing well in advance. Your goal is to be sure you know everything you need to know, have practiced so many moves in order to know how to play your best in the game, have studied, practiced, and done all you can possibly do to be at your very best when the day of the event arrives. Now, you're ready.

It's the same here where Jesus is telling us to be ready. Have you read your bible? Do you know AND understand the Scriptures? Have you done your best to live according to God's will by loving your neighbor, being helpful, serving others, being a good spouse and getting involved with your children's lives? Are you praying daily, attending worship and church, and living the life Jesus calls us all to live? If so, you are prepared so it doesn't matter what day or time Jesus comes back, you are ready to go. If you haven't been doing much or any of those types of things, you run a big risk of Jesus not recognizing you. You don't want that to happen. So, get yourself ready. Read your Bible, pray, fellowship, attend church, put what you learn into practice, turn your back on sin as best you can and when you fall, and you will, repent, ask God's forgiveness, and try again. Whatever you do, get ready, because we don't know when Jesus will return. Only that He will and we don't want Him to catch us napping.

"This is the day the Lord has made. Rejoice! And be glad in it." Smile – those prepared don't need luck. Now get out there and make this a Power Day.

2 Corinthians 5: 7 NIV: "We live by faith, not by sight."

Some versions of the Bible say "We *walk* by faith...." If you were to do the word study, you'd find that 'walk' and 'live' in this case come from the same Greek word. So, what does it mean for us to live or walk by faith, not by sight? Let me attempt an analogy that will, hopefully, clarify this for us.

You wake up in the morning and while you're having a cup of coffee, you tune into your favorite local station to hear the weather and traffic reports to find out what it's *really* like out there. The reporter says the skies are clear but it's breezy and you should take a jacket with you because the air is chilly. There are no traffic accidents or delays to report. Armed with this wonderful news, you prepare to leave for work and while putting on your suit coat, you are confident that you've done your research and 'just know' a pleasant trip to the office awaits you. So far, you have not been outside. You do not have any firsthand knowledge that it's clear but chilly. You have not yet been driving on the highways and byways, so you are fully trusting the reporter's word that everything is okay. You go anyway. You head out, merrily on your way, *in faith*, based entirely on the word of another. Up to this point, *you have not seen* anything but the inside of your home.

You and I were not there when Jesus roamed the countryside preaching and teaching. We weren't there when He healed the blind man or chased demons out of a sick man. We weren't there when He was tried or tortured. We never saw with our own eyes when they hung Jesus on the tree or got a glimpse of the empty tomb on the Third Day. We never got to witness for ourselves any or all the great things He accomplished. All we have is a book that makes a lot of incredible claims about Jesus and the many wonderful things He did and who He really is. We have the word of our parents and pastors and maybe some Sunday school teachers. We have history and archaeology and Scripture to act as proof, if we choose to believe it, but we never saw any of that for ourselves. Yet, we believe it all. We trust God, sight unseen, and believe what God's word says based on the reports of others. And because of that, life shows us some pretty amazing, wonderful, challenging, sometimes frightening and exciting things to reward and strengthen our faith.

Is faith real? I believe it is, but you must decide for yourself. Ask yourself this: what would my life be like if I didn't have my faith? How would I cope without it? Today, take a deeper look at your walk - at your life - and see more clearly just how important and magnificent your faith really is. You might be surprised.

"This is the day the Lord has made. Rejoice! And be glad in it." Smile - Live confidently...with faith in your heart. Now get out there and make this a Power Day.

Consider This:

"To climb higher on the ladder, one begins by stepping on, learning to respect and being grateful to the bottom rungs, without which, ascension isn't possible." **Jeffrey D. Hill**

Unless you've spent your life under a rock, it's a sure bet you've read articles in magazines, heard news stories on the radio or television or have even seen something online talking about people who are famous, accomplished, "big shots." Often, these stories point out how "back in the day" these people slung hash, washed cars, or worked in some type of 'menial' job. Everyone starts somewhere and generally speaking, that 'somewhere' isn't even close to the top.

Think back to those days when you were still in high school, or maybe you had just graduated, and you landed that first job that actually paid you. That job was likely something along the lines of a stocker at a grocery store or flipping burgers at a fast-food place or maybe your collected garbage or dug ditches. Everyone starts somewhere. My first pay came from doing all sorts of odd jobs for people. I painted fences, worked a lot with a shovel, carried stuff for other people and spent a lot of time in the sun doing hard physical labor in return for the much-appreciated few coins that went into my pocket. Fifty cents an hour was big bucks back in the '60's and, full disclosure, I was only 11 and the money was a foreign currency as I lived overseas, but hey - everyone starts somewhere. As much as we all like to imagine ourselves behind an important desk in the corner office of the Executive Suite, somebody has to do the work of parking cars, waiting tables, doing all sorts of manual labor, being the "gofer" at work, sorting stacks of mail in the company basement, or running errands. These are the kinds of jobs that no one aspires to, but everyone does for whatever reason. Maybe they're working their way through school or maybe, they just need the money or the experience. Regardless of the reason, we all started somewhere to "get a foot in the door." When you start on the lowest rung and work your way up, you learn far more than bypassing that first step. You learn to appreciate processes. You gain understanding and wisdom for what successful operation means. The experience helps build you into the wiser, better, more effective leader you will one day become.

Unless someone is well-connected, like the son or daughter of the business owner, there are simply not too many people who start at the top. A bit of homework reveals the fact that even fewer who start at the top, stay there very long. About the only way one comes out of high school or college straight into a CEO position is the self-employed student. That's rare.

David's dad owned the place and he had built a good business. The only mistake David's dad made was that he never made David start on the bottom rung of this ladder to success. Dad wrongly believed such a thing was "beneath" his son. The day finally came when it was time for David to take control of his dad's ladder. David never learned and had no idea why the lower rungs were there and, no surprise, he didn't know why or how to appreciate them. For the lack of that knowledge and skill, it wasn't long before David's actions caused the whole business to fall to pieces. In only four months, David destroyed the business his dad invested decades of his heart and soul into building.

The lower rungs of the ladder serve an important purpose. They are the foundation that offers learning and understanding of how all the parts make up the whole so the whole system works. They're the same reasons a child first crawls, then toddles, then walks, and running is the last step. It's a necessary process and that process, when traveled with faith, diligence, and obedience develops into what we call 'success.'

Jesus began His human experience as a baby. We all did. Do you really think that's a coincidence? Everyone starts somewhere. Don't just remember that fact of life; also remember why - and appreciate it.

"This is the day the Lord has made. Rejoice and be glad in it." Smile - As you climb your ladder, find balance and appreciate every rung. Now get out there and make this a Power Day.

Job 1:20: "The Lord gave, and the Lord has taken away; may the name of the Lord be praised."

The short version of what we know as Job's first test goes something like this: Satan's looking to cause trouble. God, after a fashion, challenges the devil by saying Job "is blameless and upright, a man who fears God and shuns evil." The devil takes the bait, accepts the challenge and the test is set. In one day… one day…the devil uses different people to steal Job's oxen and donkeys, burn his sheep, and kill his servants. As if that's not enough, the wind blows a house down, crushing to death all of Job's kids. On top of that, fire falls from the sky and burns up even more animals and servants. Boom! Just like that, it's all gone. Job is literally wiped out. Everything Job had spent his life doing and building, his family, his staff, his businesses – all of it – gone in one day. Job was devastated. What was the very first thing Job said about all of that as he wept in utter grief? "The Lord gave, and the Lord has taken away; may the name of the Lord be praised." **Score:** God 1, Satan, zip, zero, nada!

Even in the midst of this enormous tragedy and his deep sorrow and anguish, Job ran to and submitted himself to God's authority and sovereignty. No, Job didn't do that later. It wasn't after he came back to his senses. He didn't wait until he had calmed down enough to where he could cope a little better. No! Job said this right away! They were _THE_ first words out of his mouth. It is my fervent prayer that you and I never have to endure such a test at any time in your life but if we do, I pray we have the right stuff like Job to have our first act be to run to God's loving arms and submit ourselves to Him.

Perhaps just for the fun of it, or to drag this test out longer than necessary, the enemy saw to it that things got worse for Job for a goodly while before they ever got any better. I know we all have challenges. We all have defining moments in our lives that demand a decision to do something with our faith. **Honest question:** Have you had something bad happen in your life and instead of your first words to God being words of submission, were they words of blame? "How could you do this to me? You're not keeping your promises! Why did I trust you? Oh, woe is me…." If we're willing to be totally honest, I'm betting the answer is _yes_.

Why do we do that? For some unexplainable reason, many of us forget that God is God. Our focus immediately falls on self instead of Him. He created us. He owns us. He bought us for a blood price through the work of the cross. We humans tend to get so attached to "our" stuff (idols) and the people in our lives. It is a mistake to think of all that as "ours." Just a reminder – nothing actually belongs to us....every bit of it belongs to God. (**1 Cor. 10:26**) A pastor I knew years ago once put it this way: "Close your eyes. Everything you see with your eyes closed is yours to keep. Everything else belongs to God." When challenges come, and they always do, there will be time for appropriate mourning and grieving. But remember, God is still on the throne and He is doing a new and better work in your life. Grieve, yes, but also give praise and thanks. In the end, Job got it all back and then some and he was still praising God for it. Job never kicked God off the throne of his heart. Don't you, either. No matter what comes your way today or everyday....God first, especially when it hurts the worst, and the walk gets really tough.

"This is the day the Lord has made. Rejoice! And be glad in it." Smile - Faith... it'll test you. Stand ready. Now get out there and make this a Power Day.

Something to Ponder:

Proverbs 17: 17, "A friend loves at all times, and a brother is born for adversity."

Throughout the Bible, God shows us everything we need to know about both what a good and true friend is as well as how to recognize and guard against false friends. He teaches us all about the users, the deceivers, the liars, and what a phony is like and how to avoid them. Mohammed Ali once correctly observed that friendship is not taught in public schools or at most secular private schools. However, I will claim that if you attend a good Bible teaching church and Sunday school; listen closely to your pastor's sermons, get involved with a good small group, or tune into any of a host of worthy Christian writers and speakers, it's hard not to get highly educated on this topic of friendship. Friendship is, indeed, one of the best and most vital tools all of us should have in our set of life skills.

What do you know about friends and friendship? Are you aware that in their lifetime, most men will have only 1 to 3 truly close friends? Men will have any number of acquaintances and a slew of "friends" we see only on occasion, but as a general rule, we'll have just a few really close friends. On the opposite side of the gender coin, women will have many more friends and there will be multiple levels of each. It seems as though almost every other friend is her best friend. I can attest that "back in the day," the number of best friends my mother had could populate a small town....like Chicago... or Miami. I often wondered if there was anyone my mother didn't know...... everything about. I'm kidding but the point is that for women, friends (and shoes) are in seemingly endless supply.

For us men: it's two pairs of shoes, two pals and we are good to go. Women are far more relational, and the friends know A LOT about each other. Men, on the other hand, are very picky about whom they open up to about anything. When a man does go to that level of openness, it is a very big deal. "The wounds of a friend are trustworthy..." **(Pvbs 27:6)**. If you betray that hard-earned trust, God help you. To most men, a true friend is someone who, without hesitation or question, can be completely trusted, relied upon and who will gladly lay down his life for his friend should the need arise.

"There's no greater love than this, that someone would lay down his life for his friends." (**John 15:13**)

A woman will do likewise...for her kids and maybe even her husband. For her friends? Maybe. It depends. Most men naturally get a gut feeling almost instantly about whether another man can be trusted or should be kept at arm's length. That's why, Ladies, your man will often stand, puff his chest, narrow his eyes and tense his muscles the second a stranger approaches you or your children. It might only take a split second and you might not even notice, but the radar is always active and it's always accurate. Men are hard wired to protect and do battle so we instinctively know who's a friend, who's friendly, and who poses a threat. Today, now you know a bit more about Godly friendship and what God says about friends. Do your best to be a friend to others. True friends don't ask for or expect anything in return. Decide for yourself who your friends will be...and who won't. It's a big deal.

"This is the day the Lord has made. Rejoice! And be glad in it." Smile - The best way to gain a friend is to be one. Now get out there and make this a Power Day.

NOTES

Philippians 2:4: "Everyone should look out not only for his own interests, but also for the interests of others."

It is often very easy to scan over a verse like this and dismiss the message by saying, "Oh sure! I guess I'm supposed to remember it's not all about me and it's important that I pay attention to other people, too." That's a nice "Sunday school" type of answer but we would be wise to look closer. When we do, we see the verse goes a bit deeper. It presses in, as they say.

Think about it. When we look out for our own interests *and* the interests of others, we are being attentive to all sides of the same issue. If you think back, perhaps you'll recall a key lesson in basic algebra which dictates that whatever do you do on one side of an equation, you must also do to the other. The Apostle Paul is pointing out our need to not only find but maintain balance in our lives. And that takes us even deeper still. It reminds us that if we are to achieve balance, we must spend at least, if not more, equal time putting others ahead of ourselves. In other words, we are called to be like-minded in Christ.

In case that last statement had a negative effect on you and started filling your heart with fear and dread; know that being like-minded in Christ does not mean we're all little robotic duplicates of each other who think exactly the same way on every issue all the time. God is in favor of ....stick with me now.... diversity. It's just what God means by diversity is not at all the same as the what the world would have us believe. God created each one of us unique. Being like-minded in Christ simply directs us to treat each other with love, respect, dignity, and honor and so forth. One need not sacrifice one's individuality to accomplish the simple goal of loving our neighbor as ourselves.

Some Christian churches baptize babies, and some Christian churches simply dedicate them, insisting the child be at least mature enough to understand the true significance of baptism. That's not a bad thing. Some Believers sprinkle while others, who believe in the same God and read the same Bible, say proper baptism requires a full dunking. Some insist on organ music and traditional hymns while others worship just as deeply to more contemporary tunes played on guitars. We can be like minded in how we care for each other, adhere to the same standards of behavior to which God has called us, and still be diverse in our opinions about a number of matters. So, when Paul says we need to *ALSO* look out for the interests of others, he's saying we need to respect opinions that may not agree with our own - especially when those opinions bring honor and glory to God. We don't have to agree with everyone on every issue in order to be acceptable in God's eyes because we are all unique and have unique ideas and opinions. We do have to treat everyone with the same love, mercy, respect, and dignity that Christ would. Today, and every day, that's a good thing to do.

"This is the day the Lord has made. Rejoice! And be glad in it." Smile - Don't just remember the "Golden Rule." Live it. Now get out there and make this a Power Day.

Psalm 116:7: "Return to your rest, my soul, for the Lord has been good to you."

The psalmist had been through some tough times. While we don't know exactly what happened, we know those events were extreme and in this psalm we see thanksgiving. Through all those tough times, he was able to see God's hand at work and feel the presence of the Almighty. And now, on the back side of all that trouble, he recognized Who got him through it and he found peace in the Lord.

How is your day or week going? Have you - are you - facing challenges and trials? Are you tired and soul weary? Look around carefully and see where "the Lord has been good to you." I know it may not feel like it, but you can know how He's been good to you. How can you know He's been good to you? You're still here. You're okay. Yes, it may have been tough but those things that needed to get done, got done. Now, you get to return to your rest.

It truly is okay to acknowledge the reality that life has its tough days. There's no shame in that. In the tenth verse of this Psalm, the writer said he 'believed even when he was severely afflicted.' Saying those words shows his faith is strong despite the trials. He knows, in his heart, in his soul and in his mind, that God is with him. He's just saying, 'This is a tough time and I'm tired. But thank you, God, for being there.' He did what you and I need to do in tough days: Call it what it is and remember God is there for us.

I heard a young lady, a doctor, speak in a church one night. She had spent considerable time serving with a mission, doing what she could to render help to the sick and needy in Haiti. We sometimes have the arrogance to think we have it rough. But what we consider "rough" is compared only to the easy life we're used to living. We really don't have it rough and probably don't even understand what "rough" really looks like. Living outside in a makeshift tent, exposed to elements and the many different insects, having no plumbing, no sanitation, no resources, while facing disease, death and crime everywhere every day with little food and no way to help yourself – that is rough. If we've never lived through a situation like that, it's very hard, and a bit unfair, to claim we've had it rough. Yet this young doctor told of how people in those circumstance would sing God's praises every day and every night, all day long. They had it rough. They acknowledged that they had it rough. Still, they praise God and believe in Him and rely on Him. And in so doing, rest returns to their soul for the Lord has been good.

How much more so you and I? God is with us. Rely on Him. You can rest in the comfort of knowing that He is there, protecting, guiding and available for you. Rest.

"This is the day the Lord has made. Rejoice! And be glad in it." Smile - Rest for your soul begins with trust in God. Trust Him. Now get out there and make this a Power Day.

"The man convinced against his will is of the same opinion still." **A Maxim**

Many years ago, I was a 15-year-old cadet at a military school in a small town in North Georgia. One afternoon, I had an opportunity to go into the town courtesy of a short, half-day pass. I was walking on a sidewalk, taking in the sights, enjoying the beautiful weather and a bit of freedom. As I was walking, a Christian "evangelist" approached me on the sidewalk, got inches from my face and loudly asked if I was Believer. Startled, I managed only to say, "Well...." when he grabbed my shoulders, shoved me against the wall of a building, and literally yelled at me about my sins, my need to repent, that I was going to hell, how I needed God in my life and so forth. If his intention was to scare me half to death, he more than succeeded. However, his efforts did nothing at all to create in me any desire, or the sense that I needed to, repent. In truth, I admit I would have been only too happy to rearrange this guy's face but as quickly as he appeared, he stopped yelling, glared at me, and left. The only real change to my opinion was "If this is how God's people behave, I don't need it." Listen: scare tactic messages, imparted in similar awful ways to others, happens far too often. If you are of that mindset, Stop it! It doesn't work and that is decidedly NOT how Jesus taught us to share His word.

Christians can sometimes by the worst offenders and highest barriers to others who would otherwise come to know Christ and gain salvation. Mahatma Gandhi once made this point: "I would have become a Christian, but then, I met one." The fact that a deacon in a church in India turned Mahatma Gandhi away from attending that church could well be the reason India is predominately Hindu and not Christian, today. **Fact:** God has never called us, nor would He ever call us, to be rude, obnoxious, overbearing, or to lord it over anyone. To the contrary, He always calls us to "love one another." He calls us to daily practice the fruits of the spirit found in **Galatians 5:22** – "love, joy, peace, patience, kindness, goodness, faith, gentleness and self-control."

Yes, Jesus always spoke the truth. Yes, Jesus was always direct and up front. Yes, Jesus always was respectful, bold, and unashamed of the Word. His word. But He would never grab people on the street and yell at them to get them to believe. He never brow beat them into His way of thinking. He didn't humiliate or coerce. He invited. He answered questions. He reasoned with people. In quiet strength He was gentle, calm, and took time to help others understand. He didn't condemn - He taught.

No matter what we do or say, you and I will never convince anyone to change their heart. That's not our role in saving souls. All we can, or should, do is plant seeds of hope and share the answer for the hope we have (**1 Peter 3:15**) gently and with respect. It's the job of the Holy Spirit to change hearts and convict people. Whose job? The Holy Spirit's. News Flash! You and I are ***NOT*** the Holy Spirit. Maybe it is wiser to not try to convict and convince or ram God down anyone's throat. Rather, it's more likely to be a good thing if we just do what Jesus told us to do. Be nice. Be kind. Be gentle and respectful and always have an answer for the hope we have. God will do the rest. Don't throw anyone up against a wall. Don't yell. Don't badger or put unbiblical, unreasonable demands on anyone. Just be the kind of Christian who mimics Jesus and invite, teach, answer questions, help promote understanding, be bold, be honest, be helpful and set a good example. Sound like a plan? Okay, go do that.

"This is the day the Lord has made. Rejoice! And be glad in it" Smile - Kindness works. Now get out there and make this a Power Day.

Isaiah 43:19: "See, I am doing a new thing! Now it springs up; do you not perceive it? I am making a way in the desert and streams in the wasteland."

Look at this verse. Who is doing a new thing? God is. Where is He doing it? In the desert and the wastelands. What is He doing? Bringing forth water and something that we perceive is "springing up." What do you think that something is? Right! It's new life! Much like the *Enterprise* from Star Trek, God makes it possible for us to courageously go into the unknown, uncharted territory on a mission of hope and Godly purpose.

Okay, so maybe you find yourself among that group of people who, due to some personal circumstance or the effects of a bad economy, find themselves in a situation or place that bears a strong resemblance to a desert. A wasteland. No matter where you look, all you can see are the miles and miles of nothing but more miles and miles. It's desolate, barren, dry, and oppressively hot. What little breeze there is might be blowing jagged shards of sand that sting your face. What you see is a desert. Your perception is that of a wasteland. You wonder who in their right mind would ever want to be out here. It's lonely, kind of scary, it's empty and there seems to be no resource for needed provisions and you wonder how long you're going to be here. But that's your vision from human eyes and human understanding and human emotions.

Would you like to have an idea of what God sees? Imagine Rembrandt looking at a new, blank canvas. It isn't a little canvas, though. This thing is huge. You can almost see the many ideas scurrying around behind His creative eyes. In front of him is a blank canvas but his eyes see more than just an empty, desolate area. He sees a foundation upon which to build something new. He takes up his pallet in his left hand while in his right the brushes rest easily. Rembrandt's skilled hand caresses a tool as only He can and carefully, deliberately, painstakingly, and with a passion and purpose He begins to work. From that work comes something new. Something beautiful is born and begins to take form. That's God in your desert. You are the paintbrush. He's going to create something altogether different and vibrant and exciting...... with you. He will transform your wasteland into something with streams of opportunity and great pathways teeming with new life. All you have to do is your part.....go boldly into God's plan for your life.

If that's you, take heart this day. You are not captive to desolation and your perceived vast expanse of emptiness is not your home. Rather, you're on the threshold of a great, new opportunity and the Master Artist is about to make something brand new in and for your life. *You* are how He will accomplish it. Get excited! You get to do something that has never been done...and that something will come directly from God Himself! He does the work – you get the benefit. Why? Because He loves you. You have to admit, that's pretty amazing.

"This is the day the Lord has made. Rejoice! And be glad in it." Let your heart smile because today and every day you stand on the brink of the new and the great. Just be God's tool. Now get out there and make this a Power Day.

Ponder This:

"Stand still and silently glance at the world as it goes by....and undoubtedly, it will." **Anonymous**

I like to exercise my brain in various ways and one of the fun ways I do that is by solving cryptograms. The quote at the top of this page was one of those cryptograms and it stuck out to me. It reminded me of the Parable of the Good Samaritan found in **Luke 10: 25 – 37** which gave rise to a question that seemingly came from nowhere. The question was simply this: What are you going to do about it?

The quote implies there is a choice we must all make. Namely, get involved with life or more specifically, get involved in *your* life, OR, you can watch as life passes you by and you miss it altogether. Okay, oww! But that's true, isn't it? Either we're doing or we're watching or we're not even there. Of course, it's good that we cannot be, and don't have to be involved in everything, but all of us need to be involved somehow in something in our own life.

Then the question comes again - What are you going to do about it? In the "Good Samaritan" situation, there were people who walked past an injured man on the road. Some "holy men" deliberately turned a blind eye. Pious men made excuses. Learned men who knew better ignored what was right there in front of them. Then along comes the Samaritan. Of all who came by, he was the one most unlikely to offer help, but he went out of his way to get involved. He did not just do *something* - but *everything* he could do to help a stranger. He willingly gets involved in things Samaritans would normally never even consider, much less do! The others merely watched. They ignored and excused away their chance to show love and mercy; to help and live out a major facet of the life to which we Christians are called.

There are "Do-ers." **James 1:22** reminds us "Do not merely listen to the word, and so deceive yourselves. Do what it says!" There are "Watchers." It's been said there are three types of people in this world. Those who make things happen, those who watch what happens and those who wonder what happened. Have you ever noticed that those who only watch and wonder complain more often and louder about what happened than those who get involved and actively do something?

Their complaints are born of ignorance and laziness. They might say, "Somebody ought to _____." Fill in the blank with whatever you wish. Guess what?! *You* are somebody! Why don't *you* do it? Or they'll lament, "Someone should give that fellow a hand." Do a quick survey. How many hands do you have to give? You've heard them say, "Why don't the powers that be do _____instead?" Good question! Why don't you get on down to City Hall and ask them yourself? Better yet, you have a brain that works – come up with an answer to your own question and make it happen. Of course, there's the standard, "Someday, I'm gonna _____." Oh, really? Are you? Today is someday. What are you waiting for?

Listen, Friend, right now, today, you have everything you need to accomplish whatever needs doing. The only thing stopping you, is you. It's your life. You can live your life or you can stand back and watch as life passes you by. It's your choice. But you need to remember....it's *your* choice. So...what are *you* going to do about it?

"This is the day the Lord has made. Rejoice! And be glad in it." Smile - "I have come that you may life in abundance." What are going to do about that? Now get out there and make this a Power Day.

NOTES

2 Tim 2:15: "Do your best to present yourself to God as approved, a workman who does not need to be ashamed and who correctly handles the word of truth."

Now that's some good advice from the Apostle Paul. How would you suppose one might go about making that happen? Does it mean we have to work harder? Work longer? Do we have to try to be a perfectionist....even if we're not one?

You might agree it will require some thought to discover how *best* to present yourself as "a workman who does not need to be ashamed..." That thought process may take some time but when they figure that out, they can formulate a plan for the how, where, when and why part before they actually do anything. Wisdom dictates that with a plan to follow, work quality would be higher, productivity greater, and it would probably get done faster. A good plan to follow reduces the chances for mistakes. All of that together can result in a host of benefits. Having a plan seems better than just rushing in without one. The plan is the hard part.

"Think first" was one of the lessons pounded into me earlier in my own life. For me, that was a great lesson because by nature, I could lay claim to being the all-time champion poster child for impulsive people. Even today, I still need occasional reminders. It has been suggested, and rightly so, that a master of any discipline first allows his mind and eyes to reflect on a task at hand long before he ever puts his hand to it.

I have had the occasion and the honor to meet some truly great martial artists who "think first" extremely well. If you look closely, you can see in their eyes they have the entire sparring match already envisioned before they ever raise a hand. They see it first. Likewise, artists, architects, engineers, managers, and entrepreneurs take the time to think things through before they actually engage in the hands-on work. God does that for us long before we are born. "Your eyes saw me when I was formless; all my days were written in Your book and planned before a single one of them began." **Psalm 139:16**

When planning is done and in place, and one follows the plan, success generally follows. When that process is skipped, all too often, failure is not far behind. So, too, with our daily walk with God. Start your day with God in mind. See Him at work in your life, in your every step and envision His word in your work. *THEN* go take on the day. You'll find your efforts are more productive, you'll make greater progress, and your heart will be calmer through the day. Just remember the motivation from the last sentence of **Colossians 3:24**, "It is the Lord Christ you are serving." Make this a fantastic day....think first....meditate on God....go get it.

"This is the day the Lord has made. Rejoice! And be glad in it." Smile - Meditate on God's word and life just gets better. Now get out there and make this a Power Day.

Jeremiah 6:16: "This is what the Lord says: Stand at the crossroads and look; ask for the ancient paths, ask where the good way is and walk in it, and you will find rest for your souls."

I did leave off the last line of this verse for now on purpose. It never ceases to amaze me how much message God can pack into just a handful of words. It is important to look in this verse at the several things God asks us to do and silently suggests we make a decision and take action.

The first thing He tells us to do is "stand at the crossroads." Then He directs us to look. Perhaps that will remind you of a caring father teaching his child how to safely cross a street and learn something about picking a safe direction. "Johnny, before you cross the street, stop and stand on the sidewalk. Look both ways and make sure no cars are coming." Sound like a good lesson? Third, we are encouraged to "ask about the ancient ways." Does that sound a bit odd?

Let's return to the analogy. "Dad, why do we do it this way?" That's exactly the same thing. Asking why we do it this way is the equivalent of asking, "which is the way to what is good?" He gives us the answer and the answer is clear. If we stop first and look to make sure no traffic is coming, then we can cross the street and not get squished like a bug on someone's front bumper. It's safe. We do this because it is an ancient way that has proven true. It works.... every time. That's good, right? Right. Do this and you'll be far ahead of the people this verse was talking about. You see, the last line of this verse says, "But you said, 'We will not walk in it'." They made a bad choice. They gave up the benefits of obedience. Don't let that be your choice. You be wise and choose to follow God's direction.

You made a good choice and did those three things and came to a better decision. You looked and saw and asked and now you know. You see it is safe. You obtained wise counsel and are assured this is the good way. The decision is: "I will go that way." Finally, with the decision having been made, the action is simply to do it. Get up off your good intentions, put feet to your faith, and go that way.

Apply that line of thinking to everything in your life. Especially in your spiritual life because...no brainer time....Jesus is the way! Stop, look, investigate, gain wisdom and knowledge, decide, act on the decision. Result: Obedience to God provides safety, helps with good choices, offers worthy challenges, and leads to abundant living. Cool, huh? You gotta love how God makes that so simple, too.

"This is the day the Lord has made. Rejoice and be glad in it." Smile - Never stop looking for what the good way is. Now get out there and make this a Power Day.

Something to Ponder:

"What soap is to the body - laughter is to the soul."
Yiddish Proverb
Proverbs 17:22a, "A joyful heart is good medicine...."

Heart - soul....same thing, right? Someone famous, I think it was Milton Berle, said something along the lines of having "a good laugh is like taking an instant vacation." People just feel better after they laugh. If you think about it, it makes sense. There's nothing like a good laugh to clear out the fog of doubt, lift away the burden of worry and blow away the pains of the day. Don't you just feel better after a good laugh?

I've often wondered if that verse was the inspiration for Reader's Digest entitling that one section of their publication - "Laughter is Good Medicine." In my own experience, it doesn't seem to matter how far down in the dumps someone might be, if you can get them to laugh at something...anything... they generally perk up even if it's just a little bit. And as we know from the old adage; "A little bit can go a long way."

Maybe you can remember a time when you, or your kids or friends, were feeling upset because you had a great adventure planned for the day and something happened to spoil the day. The storm cancelled out the camping trip or the big event got delayed when someone came down ill. At seemingly just the right moment, somebody else came along and did or said something that magically put a brighter, cheerier light on the situation. They probably used humor, right? It's not foolproof but more often than not, it works. The thing about humor is that it has a quality that almost forces the one who is mad or sad to try and stay mad. Kids have this down to an art form and they just seem to come by this naturally as they use it on their parents all the time.

When she was still a little girl, my youngest daughter would sit by me as I tried my best to be the serious dad around the cutest angel face in the entire world and explain to her what she had done wrong and how things should be done. She would sit patiently and kind of listen as she acted like it was just another routine conversation. When I stopped talking, she would reach up and grab my cheeks, smile and say, "Daddy, you lub me 'cause I am ir-re-vist-able." I can be pretty tough but when faced with that, I melted immediately. She was right; I couldn't resist. If I didn't know better, I would think it was a plot to keep dad off balance but ....nnnaaahhhh.

Sometimes, if we can find a way to laugh at the funny side of life, it somehow becomes easier to deal with situations and we actually make better decisions. Laughter helps us forget, even for a moment, that parts of life can be daunting. It gives us strength. God's idea is "A joyful heart is good medicine....." and there's nothing like a good laugh to cure a sour disposition. Today....just laugh a little.

"This is the day the Lord has made. Rejoice! And be glad in it." Smile- Now get out there and make this a Power Day.

Proverbs 13:4: "The slacker craves, yet has nothing, the diligent is fully satisfied."

At some point in our lives, most of us have met that person who talks loud and long about what they want, what they would like to do, what they need or have done and so forth, but they never seem to have anything to show for all their talk.

That same guy is always looking for the next "big score." For some reason, he never seems to have enough money. Somehow, she is always trying to reach the next level. Ask them what they're doing to reach that level or earn any of what they say they want, and the response is always one or more of these three things: They list all the reasons why they "can't." Or, they discuss the details of who and what is to blame. Or, they'll offer an elaborate description of the barriers they've run into that make life so hard. Those are all excuses to justify (at least in their minds) why they never turned dream into reality.

Outwardly, you might just heave a sigh but inwardly, you may be thinking something that has little to do with sympathy or empathy and you might have to ask God's forgiveness later for thinking that. If you ever were that person, you would likely have a lot to tell that person....in a very loving manner, of course. Slackers talk a lot. Sadly, talking is about all they do. We've all met him...or her.

Compare and contrast that guy with the one who actually accomplishes things. This is the guy who doesn't say much about what they've done simply because they're busy working, getting more done. This is the guy who loves his work and is not arrogant, but confident enough to let his work speak for itself. He doesn't need to draw attention to himself. In fact, he'd probably rather avoid the limelight because he's humble. Others will notice his accomplishments and word will get out all on its own. If he needs something, he'll ask for it. Not surprisingly, awards. rewards and kudos seem to find and follow the achiever. People recognize him (or her) on the street and say nice things to them. They suddenly are being ushered to the head of the line because they did something that helped others and people are grateful. If this guy is an employee for a company, he's the one getting promoted. If he owns his own business, his company is the one enjoying steady growth. Why? He's doing.

He's overcoming. He is getting the work done and accomplishing goals. People respect that and are drawn to it.

Slackers never hear anything like that said to, or about, them. Why not? Slackers don't do much of anything. And since they don't do much, they don't get much and hence, they are constantly unsatisfied. The diligent, however, do get noticed and rewarded and "magically" find contentment. Sure, there are lots of challenges along the way. Guess who perseveres and ends up satisfied? Yep. You got it. Today...you be that one....the diligent one.

"This is the day the Lord has made. Rejoice! And be glad in it." Smile - Be diligent. Be satisfied. Now get out there and make this a Power Day.

Matthew 13:24-30: The Parable of the Wheat and the Weeds

I would encourage you today, and every day, to open your Bible and read it. Right now, I'm asking you to focus on all seven verses of this parable as it has so much value for your life today. In this story, Christ offers a great comparison and analogy about heaven using a farmer as the example. The nutshell version goes like this: The farmer plants good seed, in this case, wheat. Along comes the bad guy and tosses weed seeds into the farmer's garden and, as you would expect, both seeds grow. The servants see what is happening and tell the farmer, asking him if they should pull the weeds.

In verses 29 and 30, the farmer responds by saying, "No. When you gather up the weeds, you might also uproot the wheat with them. Let both grow together until the harvest. At harvest time, I'll tell the reapers: Gather the weeds first and tie them in bundles to burn them but store the wheat in my barn." Take a few moments and think about this and what is portrayed for us to see here.

God created earth. God planted seeds of humanity complete with all manner of goodness built into them. Satan comes along and plants weeds of sinfulness. Both seeds grow – the good and the bad. Some of the wheat is strong and thrives in spite of the weeds by holding firm to its roots. Some wheat is weaker and fails to get a grip on its roots is choked out by the weeds. The weeds thrive, too, doing what weeds do – killing what is good, producing what is bad, and just being a menace and creating havoc.

In the end, the farmer (God) will send His reapers to the harvest. Some reapers come with smiles and goodwill and escort the happy "Wheaties" to the sound of trumpets and take them to heaven. Some of those reapers are grim. Their job is to gather all the weeds...unbelievers, deniers, skeptics, the unrepentant …and throw them into the eternal fires that are unimaginably hot and never go out.

It is vitally important to pay attention to this part of the story. *The servants wanted to help save the wheat,* but the farmer said no. Why do you suppose He did that? Could it be because the farmer gave the wheat free will? Here's the lesson: *You and I have the chance to accept or decline the invitation and gift of salvation.*

There have always been, and will always be, weeds in our society. We, the wheat, live our earthly lives side by side with every variety of weed that exists. Those weeds are always ready and anxious to latch on and choke us, block out the Light, and try to destroy us. It is vital to know we need to have our roots firmly anchored in good soil. The kind of soil that holds us fast to the Creator. We drink in Living Water, gain strength from Him, and persevere until it's time to be harvested and move up to more important purposes.

Today, be encouraged to resist the weeds. Stay firmly rooted in good soil. Wheat or weed, harvest time comes for both. We all have souls that will live forever but we're not all going to the same eternity. We must focus on which eternity you truly want and fight the good fight to never let go of that.

"This is the day the Lord has made. Rejoice and be glad in it." Smile - Grow where you're planted, develop strong roots, and resist weeds because that makes for an abundant life. Now get out there and make this a Power Day.

NOTES

Something to Ponder:

"Well done is better than well said." **Benjamin Franklin**

A lot of people say many things that sound great and wonderful and seemingly make sense when we hear them. People's actions, however, don't always match their words and that is legitimate cause for us to wonder about that person. For example, during the 2008 presidential campaign, Barack Obama made numerous public announcements that his administration's dealings would be the most open and transparent ever. What was done once he was in office proved that transparency was not a priority for that administration.

A famous hockey player once publicly commented that he strove to be a man of good character and to live in an honorable manner so as not to embarrass himself or his family. A noble and worthy goal, to be sure and one most men strive to reach. Yet, certain actions by this player proved contrary to his words and his intentions when he got arrested for drunk driving and behaving badly in public. All spouses pledge undying love for their mates, yet far too many indulge in actions that are anything but faithful. "Well done is better than well said."

One of my favorite quotes which I refer to often simply says, "Deeds. Not words." **James, Chapter 2** tells us that it's great to have faith but if we only talk about it, that faith is weak. Well, full disclosure, "weak" isn't how James described it. What'd he call it? Oh yeah...DEAD! He said, beginning in **verse 17**, "In the same way, faith by itself, if it is not accompanied by action, is dead." He goes on to say in **verse 18**, "But someone will say, 'you have faith; I have deeds.' Show me your faith without deeds and I will show you my faith by what I do." In **verse 22**, James points out that Abraham combined faith **and** action. Major life lesson for all parents: One of life's glaring facts is that all children listen to what their parents DO far more intently than what their parents say.

Through many years of martial arts practice, I've had occasion to encounter those who liked to talk tough in a rather loud manner. Smack talking and trying to be intimidating. But when push came to shove, all too often, their actions failed to give their words credibility. It's the quiet ones you need to respect more. They don't talk nearly as much as they do. Jesus covered all the bases through His teachings and He backed all of it up solidly with everything He did.

This isn't to say that people are not saying anything credible or trustworthy. It's important to look closely at the relationship between what people say and what they do. Do words match actions? If they do, great! That's powerful. If they don't, Mr. Franklin is right. James is right. What we say is one thing. _What we do is a far better indicator of who and what we are._ Today, don't let your mouth write a check your actions can't cash. Say what you mean, mean what you say, don't be mean when you say it, and let your lifestyle prove your words true. "Well done is better than well said."

"This is the day the Lord has made. Rejoice! And be glad in it." Smile - Before you say it, ask yourself, "Will what I'm going to do prove what I'm about to say?" If not, ssshhhh! Now get out there and make this a Power Day.

Proverbs 6:22 HCSB: "When you walk here and there, they will guide you; when you lie down, they will watch over you; when you wake up, they will talk to you."

Huh? What will guide you? Who will watch over you, and who will talk to you? Oohhh, there it is. It's your parent's teaching. Go back up to verse 20 where Proverbs 6 tells us, "My son, keep your father's command, and don't reject your mother's teaching." Now, that makes more sense. It's not all that uncommon to hear people say...almost with a note of surprise in their voice, "Oh! I sound just like my father!" Or mother...as the case may be.

It makes perfect sense that people making such a comment really listened to their parents, learned from them, and followed their example. How else would they know what they sounded like? Hopefully, most of what they learned was good and useful. There are a lot of times when I catch myself repeating the same things my parents used to say and copying many of their behaviors. So do my siblings. Chances are you're not much different. What's kind of fun and comforting is hearing your kids repeating those same things, as well. One day, they too will say, with equal surprise..."Oh! I sound just like my dad!" Think about that for a moment and realize the thing we didn't take into account is that it's not really our parents we sound like. It's grandpa and grandma or great grandpa and great grandma or even the great-greats or further back.

You see, good advice and lessons that are truly worthwhile don't wear out. They can span generations. Maybe that's why the Holy Bible has been, not just a best seller, but _the_ best seller, every single year since it was first published. Good news, good advice, and worthwhile lessons go a very long way and truth....well, truth never changes. Truth never outlives its accuracy or usefulness.

Why is that such a phenomenon? What's the big deal? The big deal is this kind of wisdom, advice, and guidance permeates and affects literally every aspect of our life. Far better even than our parent's good advice is God's wisdom. When we become immersed in God's word and strengthen our whole relationship with God every single area of our life is guided, protected, and watched over by God.

Our goal should be to mature in our walk to the point where the only question we ask about anything new coming into our lives is, "What does God's word say about this?" Then we open our Bibles, find our answer and automatically follow that advice. We don't have to question it because we know from vast experience that God's word, His commands, and His teachings all work to the good in our lives. God is trustworthy. That's what this proverb is saying. Learn from your parents and even more so from Father God because it truly is good advice that will stand you in very good stead. You know that's it's true. Your life experience proves it. So, keep doing that and you'll have one more good reason to know that....

"This is the day the Lord has made. Rejoice and be glad in it." Smile -Just as the key to your car is the only one that works, God's word is the only working key to your having an abundant life. Now get out there and make this a Power Day.

Something to Ponder:

God created us to have needs, not counting them as sinful or selfish. Without them, we'd have no way of knowing our need for God or how much He loves us. **Anonymous**

For most of us, our earliest recollections date back to age 3 or 4 years old. Prior to that age, we went on pure instinct. When we are old enough to recall memories, we become able to learn and discover more. We realize that we need things like food and protection or help from others. We learn to rely on those who can fulfill our needs. As we learn what our needs are, we discover our wants, as well. Eventually, we even learn to know the difference between needs and wants.

I agree with Anonymous that needs are neither selfish nor sinful. Wants *can* be, but not needs. Our need for food, water and oxygen to survive is neither sinful nor selfish - merely a fact of life. Though we may deny it, we need good and meaningful relationships. None of us can do everything alone. Wants are not needs. All too often, we confuse wants and needs which inevitably creates problems in our lives. I don't need a fire engine red, $ 500,000 Ferrari in my garage. It would be very nice to have one. If you want to give me one, God bless you! But I don't need it. Unfortunately, some folks would see that as a need. It isn't.

Any parent can testify to the fact that many things young children beg and plead for are things they "need." They don't need them. They want it and if they can the parents to cave into their whiny nagging, they'll win. That's why they try. On the plus side, you've at least got to give them credit for effort and testing their sales skills. In this life, it is true that we need money to live on. It's not selfish or sinful to work hard to improve your life for good reason, with proper motives. God is not opposed to our being successful. Just remember, He gave us skills and gifts to use in the service of others and He expects us to use those gifts to the best of our ability. He wants us to recognize and remember where those gifts came from and always give Him the glory. He asks us to return a portion of our wealth to further His kingdom, help the poor, and to be generous givers. If you amass great wealth, hoard it and claim, "Look what I did!" then you're way out of line and that is, in fact, a serious sin.

Money should never be the main goal. While money is a need, it is also just a tool that should work for us. If money owns us, we have a serious problem.

So, we do have legitimate needs. Our needs tell us when to eat, sleep, get active, defend ourselves, work or to reach out to God. If we didn't know we needed God, as some don't, our lives would be empty of so many good and valuable things. We might have stuff and some friends and so on, but without fulfilling our need for God, life is just empty.

What is the key to having our needs met? I offer this for your consideration. The key to having needs met is being open to receiving. Yes, it is more blessed to give, but we also *need* to know how to receive. <u>All</u> needs can be met, but you must receive that which fulfills the need. That's not selfish and it isn't sinful. It helps us know God better. Admit it...you need God. We all do.

"This is the day the Lord has made. Rejoice! And be glad in it. "Smile - You can only be the real you with God in your life. You need Him. Go out there and make this a Power Day.

Romans 12:21: "Do not be overcome by evil but overcome evil with good."

The HCSB version uses the word 'conquered' instead of 'overcome.' I like that. What does it mean to be overcome or conquered? It means we've been beaten into submission. It means we've been so deeply affected by something or someone we feel like we can no longer resist. In this verse, it's evil that threatens to conquer and overcome us. Jesus is telling us that instead of us giving in and being defeated by evil, we can turn the tables on evil. We can be conquerors. We can overcome evil.

Here, God asks us to return kindness for insult. He says we should help those who hate us. We need to pray for and love our enemies. If they throw rocks, we catch those rocks and use them to build something useful. They call us names and we love them with God's grace and mercy. Why? If we deliberately choose to NOT respond in kind when others attack us, that attack stands alone and has no support. Trading insult for insult only generates more anger, fear, and hatred. Trading violence for violence only prolongs the violence.

Please understand I am in no way advocating for pacifism. Far from it. There are times when we've done all we can to peacefully end a bad situation, and all of that failed and the only remaining option is to stand and fight to protect your family or your nation or yourself. If that is what you must do, do it. There is nothing in God's word dictating that we must be doormats, victims or pacifists. Yes, our primary goal is to avoid or deter violence. We are told to turn the other cheek. However, we only have one other cheek to turn and after that – to stand. **(Eph. 6:13)** Punishing is not our first option. It is up to God to punish or take vengeance, not us. **(Hebrews 10:30)**. This verse in Romans is also implying that we don't sink to their level but take the high road. We need to be better than that. The high road is the courageous, and right thing to do. Face it, anybody can trade insults and punches, which accomplishes and proves nothing except you can be just like the evil guy. That's not what you want to prove, is it?

Christians are called to be different. Set apart. Not superior, not arrogant and not sitting atop our high horse; just different. What can we do differently? We can make wiser, more rational choices. We can smile in the face of anger. We can stay silent when mocked or insulted. We can avoid silly, needless confrontations. We can extend a friendly hand, anyway. We can show kindness, anyway. We can stay calm and collected, regardless. We can trust God our Father to *be* God our Father and let Him fight the battle. I'm not talking about running away or quitting anything. I'm saying identify aspects in a situation that won't work and choose instead positive, healthy options that help you be better, do better, and live better. You can boldly lay claim to what's right and work to strengthen that, too. No, it isn't easy but it is certainly different. Bonus! It brings God glory and stores up treasures for you in heaven when you make the choice to not be overcome by evil but to overcome evil with good.

"This is the day the Lord has made. Rejoice! And be glad in it." Smile – You don't have to change the evil person. You just need to let Christ shine through you. Now get out there and make this a Power Day.

Proverbs 27:19: "As the water reflects the face, so the heart reflects the person."

Have you ever looked into a mirror and wondered, "Who is that?" It's a question as old as time itself. All of us, at some point in our lives, face the questions of who we are and what we are truly all about. Entire industries have been built just on helping people find the answers to those questions. Who am I? What am I here for? It's a very big issue and many people struggle with it.

Mirrors don't lie. The mirror will give you a precise, accurate picture of how you look on the outside. We all have those times when we're alone in front of the mirror and the reflection either puts a smile on our face or elicits a less than positive reaction. We hear ourselves thinking things like, "I look really good!" "I still got it! To "I should probably cut back on the donuts." To "Oh my goodness! What happened to you?!" We try standing a little straighter, flex those muscles one more time, suck in here and stretch a bit there and, sometimes, wish we could instantly recapture the glory days of our youth when we were in better shape, less gray and wrinkle free. I don't know about you, but I can almost get to where I don't look too awful for a chunky, gray-haired, out of shape older guy who likes to imagine he's still got it. Like it or not, what you see in the mirror is what we really look like on the outside. Mirrors don't lie.

It's the same with our hearts. The bible says, "For out of the overflow of the heart, the mouth speaks." (**Mth 12:34**) Who and what we truly are flows out of our mouths in the form of our words. If you listen to yourself when you speak, you'll know who and what you are right then. It may surprise you because you'll claim to think and believe one way, but your tone and your words will offer the true picture. Do your words match your claims? Of course, we can hide our true feelings from others for a while but sooner or later, the truth will be known. Someone once said, "You can fool some of the people all the time, and all of the people some of the time, but you can't fool all the people all the time." The day always comes when our true heart is revealed.

It's like the guy who says he hasn't got a prejudiced bone in his body is the same guy you overhear later slamming others because they're this or that. The heart cannot be hidden forever. Truth always floats to the surface. That we know that is the case, why not make it easy on ourselves and just be genuine to begin with? Be who you really are all the time. Be bold and say what you really think or believe...."with gentleness and respect" as directed by God in **1 Pt 3:15.** Even if they disagree with you, others will respect you a lot more for being genuine. It is possible and fairly easy to be tactful, respectful, and polite without compromising your integrity. That's really the key, isn't it?

Today and all the days of your life, let your heat show who you truly are. Speak your mind and stand up for your beliefs. It's *your* heart and it's going to be made known anyway. Be honest. Takes guts these days but hey, God made you who are...why would you want to hide that?

"This is the day the Lord has made. Rejoice and be glad in it." Smile - God needs you to be you. Let others be someone else...because they are. Now get out there and make this a Power Day.

NOTES

Something to Ponder:

If God already knows what we need, why pray?

Let me ask you this: Is the fact that you already know the sun is going to rise in the east tomorrow morning the reason why the sun will rise in the east tomorrow morning? No, of course not.

The fact that God already knows what the future holds doesn't mean it's fatalistically determined. If you're a parent, often times you already know what your children will ask of you before they ask it. Do you stop them from asking? Probably not. Based on long experience, you already have a great idea of what your workday will be like long before you go to the office, but you get up, get dressed and go to work anyway.

There are many excellent reasons for praying to God throughout every single day. Hopefully, asking God for what you need and want is not the only reason you pray. If it is, you're missing out on a vital aspect of building a deeper and more meaningful, dynamic personal relationship with Him. In His word, God tells us that our prayers and our work produce results. They have meaning and a purpose. Praying to God is an important part of your relationship with Him just as talking with your spouse and children and other family is vital to those relationships. The fact you already know so much about them doesn't stop you from talking to them....or at least, it shouldn't.

Prayer is more than just asking God for stuff and for your needs to be met. It's listening. It's talking to Him about how you feel, what you're afraid of or excited about. Prayer is thanking God for all the things He is doing in your life. "Hey, God, what a gorgeous sunrise this morning! That was awesome!" is just as valid, important, and worthy a prayer as anything else you can pray about. Prayers can be long or short; dramatic or whimsical; deep or simple; confession or praise; worshipful and reverent or you can unload everything about your terrible, boo-bad awful day. He won't be put off, bothered, or burdened in any way by your prayers. He wants you to come to Him with every part of you and your life. He invites you to do that. Even if you're angry at Him, He says, "Come, let us reason together." (**Isaiah 1:18**)

You have an important relationship with God. It's personal. Prayer is how you communicate with Him and one of the ways you can hear Him respond. That's why you pray, anyway. Prayer is not a one-way conversation; it always a two-way thing. It's not that He already knows what you're going to ask or say but it's also that *you don't know what He's got to say until you ask Him.* Make today better - talk to God. "Pray continuously." (**1 Thes. 5:17**)

"This is the day the Lord has made. Rejoice! And be glad in it." Smile - Prayer is relationship with God. You can tell Him anything and everything. Now get out there and make this a Power Day.

Proverbs 14:15: "A simple man believes anything, but a prudent man gives thought to his steps."

Words are incredible. Fun words, deep words, descriptive words, big words, small words. It's how we communicate and learn and accomplish so many things. Here are some words to consider: Gullible. Naive. Inexperienced. Foolhardy. Impetuous. Rash. What these words have in common is they describe people who fail to think things through. Instead, they ignore facts and information they truly need, take someone else's word – even if they don't know that someone - and run headlong into a situation that could easily ensnare them in all sorts of trouble.

How many of us are in the habit of listening to only one resource for our news? If we do that, I can guarantee we're not getting the whole story. It's only one perspective. Think about it. The nightly news is only a half hour long and, in that time, we heard headlines, sports, weather, local interest topics and commercials. With all that packed into thirty minutes, there's simply no way all the facts are being reported. If that reporter or station is biased at all, (and most are) the few facts given are likely distorted or outright lies. If we believe what we hear in that situation, we've been duped and are, by definition, simple. One life lesson you can use all the time is this: There is always, always, always more to the story.

Therefore, this proverb describes each of us at some point - or points - in our own lives. There are the times we overestimate our own abilities and bite off more than we can chew. There are times we make decisions without fully knowing what we're really getting into or properly understanding the impact our decision could have on ourselves or others. We've all been there and done that. Our own memories are packed with the lessons learned from each of those events. At least, we hope they are planted firmly in our brain. Those experiences became the foundational reasons we told our own kids what to do or not do in various situations. We just kept that reason a secret from them a while longer.

A prudent person began as a simple person. A prudent man is experienced. Experience is what allows a prudent man to be sensible. A prudent man gained his education both from school and life. He is the one who has pursued wisdom and now takes the time to think things through and weigh all the pros and cons before making any decision and definitely before taking action. The impetuous man races up the steep hill to prove something that doesn't matter while the sensible man takes his time, walks up, and enjoys the scenery and notices so much more. Today, God has two words for us to remember. Think first!

"This is the day the Lord has made. Rejoice and be glad in it." Smile - God gave us all a brain. Seems like a good idea to use it. Now get out there and make this a Power Day.

Matthew 20:26 : "….Instead, whoever wants to become great among you must be your servant."

Be a servant to be great. God created you for that – to serve. You are the answer to someone's question. You are, or have, the solution to someone else's problem. There is a real need you are on planet Earth to fulfill. You are unique, one of a kind, and have what it takes to accomplish something no one else on the face of this earth can accomplish. You have a God-given purpose for your life!

I also have a purpose as does that guy over there. And her - that lady in the corner. So does this child and the policeman, the cook in the restaurant and the guy who drives that giant combine out the field. There is a reason and a purpose for the minister of that tiny country church and the lady who teaches the kids in school and the engineer who came up that idea we all thought was too wild and crazy - at first - but it turned out to be brilliant. The one thing they have in common is using their gifts to serve others. And they are great! Everyone is unique and everyone has a purpose, and the purpose is to serve.

Remember that nasty snowstorm you drove through when trying to get home and you got stuck in a ditch? God sent a person to pull you out that ditch. You remember the guy who repaired your stove and the lady who did your taxes, saving you big bucks on your return? God sent them, too. He sent the plumber, the electrician and even that doctor with the awful bedside manner but who had the right answer that got you well again. God sent the painter and the dietician, the crossing guard and the kid who protected your kid from the bully at school and the comedian who made you laugh like that for the first time in ages. Our Lord sent that one person to you who makes your heart smile every time you're near them. God sent the very special men and women who volunteered to stand against our nations' enemies, no matter the cost, so you wouldn't have to do it yourself. Let's not forget the brave and amazing people who get it done when it comes to putting out fires, saving lives, or catching the guy who wrecked your home or robbed your business. They, too, were sent to serve and they, too, are great.

God sent you and me to do our part to help ease the pain and suffering in this world. He sent us to lend a hand to those who need it, to protect and serve, to guide and build, to invent and discover and blaze one more trail. He sent me to write this to remind you that God sent you to do your thing to serve and help others. He needs you to be great - to serve. Don't wait. Don't waste time with silly questions. Do not allow anything to get in your way. You have a purpose. God sent you to fulfill that purpose. Today, now, go and find your joy in service.

"This is the day the Lord has made. Rejoice! And be glad in it." Smile - When you get down to it, problem solving is really all about serving. Now get out there and make this a Power Day.

Psalm 127:1: "Unless the Lord builds a house, its builders labor over it in vain; unless the Lord watches over a city, the watchman stays alert in vain."

Sometimes, when you go to a movie theater to see a show, there is someone who laughs or cries at all the wrong places. It's enough to make you wonder if you are watching the same movie they are. I don't know who it was that first pointed this out, but I agree with the notion that if people don't always laugh or cry at all the right spots while watching a show, it is probably wrong to blame the movie. More likely, it would be the viewer who simply doesn't get it.

That's how it is with "building a house," which translates to mean pretty much anything we do without getting the Lord fully involved. Far too often, we don't even pray about a project beforehand or even think about taking it to God first. We just go our merry way, thinking our own plans will work just fine. We figure we've got the knowledge, the tools, the location, the blueprints, and have all our issues worked out in our own plan and we are ready to go. It gets worse. By not getting God involved up front, the implication, intended or not, is we think our way is better than God's way and that we don't need Him. That's blasphemy. Blasphemy is a huge mistake no one with any sense whatsoever wants to make. How many times has our stubborn pride taken over and we hear ourselves saying...out loud, even; "I am doing this *my* way!"? Here's a life lesson: Any number above zero is too many.

God points out very clearly in this passage that going "our own way" is a one-way trip to downtown 'Futility'. Kindly notice also that this passage is very direct and up front. There's no sugar coating or political correctness here. There's no ambiguity or hidden meaning. Get this message: If God's not in it – whatever "it" is – you are flat out wasting your time. You can plan as much as you want. You can be sure you've covered every base, dotted every 'i" and crossed every 't'. You can count, recount, measure multiple times, triple check your figures and supplies, and review your plans and agendas with a fine-toothed comb. If you left God out of any part of the process, every bit of that effort is in vain.

Yes, of course, you will build a house, host an event, tackle that big project and it will look, feel, sound, and act like a good thing. But a day will come when something happens and you will need to hold it together, and it just won't hold. If the Lord is not in it, it will eventually fall apart. Obviously, the house is a metaphor for your life, your heart, and all you do in this life. If you want to find and enjoy the kind of value and worth and even success you can rely on, you need God to get there. If you want what you've worked for to be protected and to endure, you need God. If you want to build a great legacy to pass on to your heirs, you must have God in all that you do. Without Him, it's all in vain.

With God in our lives and by doing life the way He tells us, we have a promise that our efforts will produce good fruit in all areas of our life. Today, before you begin anything new or pick up where you left off last week, get God involved. "Work as unto the Lord" in all that you do. "Trust your plans to the Lord and they will succeed." **(Proverbs 16:3)**. Why? Because when you're in Christ, "your" plans are His plans, and His plan never fails. Putting God first in your life ensures your efforts will not be in vain.

"This is the day the Lord has made. Rejoice! And be glad in it." Smile -Remember - "Seek *first* the kingdom...*then*...all is added..." **(Matthew 6:33)** Now get out there and make this a Power Day.

Proverbs 29:25: "The fear of man is a snare, but the one who trusts in the Lord is protected."

If you did a word study on "protected," you would find that its original Hebrew meaning was to be "raised high." In other words, if we put our trust in God, He will keep us safe from whatever temptation or pressure happens to be our current circumstance.

At first glance, this verse may seem to be talking about being afraid of other people because of some physical reason – they're so big, so scary, or so mean. That's not what this is about. The "snare" talked about here is the fear of what we imagine could happen if we don't support or go along with the wicked, evil, or just plain wrong ideas and actions of others. What if they exclude me? What if they hate me? What if they scoff at me? What if it costs me a job? It's bondage to others due to fear and because of a lack of trust. It feels like we can't escape fear's grip. Sadly, too many understand that dilemma. Such fear, as hard as it seems, isn't the bad part. Look at the last half of the verse. It implies man is ensnared by fear because he doesn't trust God. Notice: "...but the one who trusts in the Lord is protected." Trust in God offers protection. Not trusting God is how we get trapped in worldly ways. *Snare* is a good term to use because isn't that what fear does to us? Fear makes us feel trapped - like we have no way out. We want to the right thing, but we can't. We're trapped. Fear stops us cold in our tracks. Fear blurs both our physical and spiritual vision. Blurry vision puts us on a rocky, downward path that snowballs into nothing but trouble.

Guess what? There is good news! You can be freed from your fear right now. I don't want to make light of this because it may not be easy to be set free, but it is simple. Who is the one protected? The one who trusts in God. To trust God, you must get to know Him. When you do, you can accept the only One who can control your life in a way that keeps you safe from fearful things. That One is not the bully. That One is not the bad boss nor whomever the overbearing person is in your life. The One and only One is God. He loves you. He has a plan for your life which never includes your being or feeling trapped.

When your trust is in God, fear has no place in your life. God loves us perfectly and "Perfect love casts out all fear." **(1 John 4:18)** When we are not living in fear, we remain calm and clear-headed. We make better decisions. It won't matter what the world thinks or says of us because we're living for God, not the world. Yes, life will have its challenging days and some days will be hard and scary. Some days will seem like God just took off and we'll wonder if He's there for us. He is. He's just doing something we can't see. That's where faith and trust play a stronger role. God never forgets us. Trust in the Lord. Allow Him to be in control, and things do get better. Today, understand that God is on your side and you can have no better friend or protector and with Him you can rise and soar over any situation.

"This is the day the Lord has made. Rejoice! And be glad in it." Smile - Stand up, stand firm. See clearly, fear nothing. Now get out there and make this a Power Day.

NOTES

Something To Ponder:

What is one thing you would like to learn to do and why? **Just a Question**

Life has ways of reminding us of all sorts of things as we live day-to-day. One of the more important daily reminders is this: Regardless of how much we've learned and know and understand in our lives, there is an endless supply of new things yet to be learned. There are countless things yet to do.

What is something you'd like to learn about or learn to do? It's kind of amazing when we think about all the things we've ever done and all the things we know and can do now, that there remains a massive amount we can still learn and do that we've never yet experienced. I am what you might call a "knowledge junkie." I love to learn more about anything, but my main focus points are Christian Apologetics, politics and business topics. At the same time, I think it would be fun and exciting to learn fencing, as well. I've always wanted to learn woodworking and be able to do it well. What about you? What grabs your attention?

Learning new skills and new information is exciting and always enhances our personal growth. These are the things we've not yet done or experienced and things that would increase our knowledge base and skill sets. It could be you want to experience the adventure, or feel the speed, or find out if you're up to the challenge. Perhaps you just want a thrill or explore your creativity. Maybe it's the chance to see from a different perspective, to add new meaning to life, develop new skills or just make life more interesting. But 'wanting to' is only one side of the coin, isn't it? The flip side of the coin asks the question: Why haven't we done those things? What is stopping us from learning and doing the things we really want to learn?

Let me play "Captain Obvious" for a moment and claim that the one excuse common to us all is that "Life just got in the way. I got busy with _____(fill in the blank) and time slipped away." We wonder if it is too late to even try any of those dreams. It may be true that we did get busy with other things but that is an excuse. Time does slip away but time passes regardless of what we're doing. That just means we probably need to take a closer look at our priorities. Answer the tougher question: Did time slip away because we were doing something worthwhile or did that time go to waste as we camped on the couch and stared at the television?

We must face the fact that the excuse, "It's too late" is an outright lie straight from the pit of hell. If you still draw breath and are still alive, you have the time and ability to learn to do something you've always wanted to do. _You can_. There it is; in the most direct, pure and simplest form you can get it. _You can_. We have no excuse and the only thing stopping us is ourselves. There is something you've wanted to learn to do. There is no rule requiring you to do it alone or fast or perfect or anything else. It's what you want to learn or do. Go learn or do it. Expand your life horizons! Live a little! God will smile on you when you lean more and do more of His will for your life.

"This is the day the Lord has made. Rejoice! And be glad in it." Smile - We can never learn too much. The joy is we get to choose what we learn. Now get out there and make this a Power Day.

Psalm 34:19: "A righteous man may have many troubles, but the Lord delivers him from them all."

How many and what kinds of troubles would befall a righteous man, you ask? That list is much longer than you or I could ever fully read. You may recall in **Matthew 6:34**, Jesus tells us that "every day has trouble of its own." If you do the math and multiply your age times 365 and add in an extra day for each of the leap years you've lived through, that's a lot of troubles even if you just had one a day. Most of us endure more than one per day so, at least, double that number. For me, that would be more than 50,000 counting the days with more than 2 troubles in them. Big troubles and small and everything in between. It adds up.

Even though that many troubles could or did befall you, ask yourself this: Have you lived through all of them? I'm assuming you're still alive to be reading this so it's probably okay to nod in agreement. Another question: Can you honestly look back now and laugh about some of those things? Of course, you can. It can probably also be said that when you think about some of those troubles, two things will hold true. **One:** What you thought at the time was an impossible challenge, in retrospect seems rather petty now. **Two:** If you had not experienced some of those earlier issues, you would never have been able to handle many of the later ones. It was the trouble you had at age 24 that taught you how to get through the trouble at age 30. It was your experience of "this" which gave you the wisdom and skill to handle "that." And what does God's word say in today's verse? God delivers the righteous from every single one of those troubles, no matter how many there are.

Notice something important, however. God's word *does not say* God eliminates any of the troubles nor does He promise any of us will be exempt from the troubles. His Word makes no mention of the troubles being eased or lessened in any way. It only says God will deliver us from them under the qualification that we are righteous. Not self-righteous – righteous. What is it to be righteous? It means to be in right standing with God. You have, through faith, accepted Jesus as your personal savior. God forgave your sins and declared you righteous because of what Jesus did for you. Jesus' righteousness is imputed to you by God. The fancy Christianese word is *Justified*.

Every day has its fair share of "oh my....now what?" type of stuff. Don't forget God. Trust in Him. Pray. Ask directions. Then do what God's will for you is – stay calm, think, rely on the gifts God gave you and do the right thing. You will, at some point, be delivered from the trouble. It will enhance your life in good and surprising ways. Do that today and be ready to be amazed at what happens.

"This is the day the Lord has made. Rejoice! And be glad in it." Smile - The challenge is to trust God most when it seems like He's not around. He is. He delivers. Now get out there and maximize your day.

Something to Ponder:

"The best way to multiply happiness is
to divide it." **Source Unknown**

Perhaps you have had those times when you're alone and something happened
in your life that made you happy. Let's say you got a card in the mail from
a friend and inside the card is picture of that friend and it made you happy
to see it. A little while later, if you're still alone, that sense of happiness does
not go away but it subsides a bit. Still, you're thinking it was a good day
for having received that card and picture. But you're not going to spend all
afternoon looking at the picture. Well, you might but that's....kind of like....
well, anyway.... So, my point is you're happy for a while and then you calm
down.

Then your spouse and other family comes home and after the normal 'hello's'
and 'how was your day' stuff, you get excited again! "Oh, look at this new
picture of my friend! Don't they look great?!" You get all happy again. Why?
You get to relive the moment when you first opened the envelope. But you're
also sharing that joy and you'll find your joy has even multiplied. It is entirely
possible that your spouse and family are just as happy as you are about the
card and picture of your friend.

Happiness is multiplied because you shared it. In math world, when one
divides something, that only makes it smaller. That's not always the case.
In the world of business, it sometimes happens when one company buys
out another company the new owners will divide the acquisition and do
something different with the parts because there's more value and production
that way. It's a good investment tactic that brings greater prosperity and new
opportunity for all involved, including any sold units. The same is true of
happiness. Sharing happiness makes it bigger and better.

Divide and multiply! Hey, it works! That's how families grow. The kids leave
home, marry, have kids of their own and so on. Cities section off new ground
and expand their territory. Companies' open offices or branches in multiple
locations to grow and prosper. Share and happiness expands. Have you ever

known anyone to reject happiness when it's offered to them? Me, either. Happiness is multiplied when you divide it. Today....share your joy!

"This is the day the Lord has made. Rejoice! And be glad in it." Smile - Divide and multiply is why giving is always better than receiving. Now get out there and make this a Power Day.

Romans 12:2: "Do not conform any longer to the pattern of this world but be transformed by the renewing of your mind. Then you will be able to test and approve what God's will is – His good, pleasing, and perfect will."

Simply put, "*this world*" is where God is unaccepted and despised. It is where sin abounds unchecked. The *world* offers easy access to all manner of sexual immorality, crime, strife, treachery, unwarranted violence, abortion, good being called evil as evil is celebrated as good, and so on. The *world* asks us to agree evil things are perfectly okay when we know they are not. The *world* is the devil's playground. Sure, there are good things in the world, too, the flowers among the weeds. Christians say, "we are in the world, but not of the world." We live in the same world as everyone else, but this is not our 'forever home' so, as best we can, we avoid conforming to evil and sinful things. It is vital to understand this approach doesn't stem from a "holier-than-thou" attitude or a sense of superiority. It's not pride or arrogance. We should never look down on anyone because all people are sinners who've fallen short of God's glory. 'All' includes us so none of us are qualified to "cast the first stone." There are two main reasons we avoid conforming to the world. First and foremost, God told us not to so out of love, respect and obedience to the One who is Lord, we live to honor Him. Second, it's plain ol' common sense. *Worldly* things have no value for anyone. The world turns a blind eye to adultery, but no one rejoices over a spouse betrayed. The same worldly woman who says murder is always bad might willingly visit an abortion clinic and participate in just exactly that act. Millions of gallons of alcohol and tons of drugs are consumed every year for "fun" but there is no group for alcoholics or drug addicts to celebrate the joys of addiction. Only groups that offer a way out of that life. Many people are trapped in crime groups, wishing they could break away. That's the *world* I speak about. It's destructive. It's painful. It's a prison. Why would anyone deliberately participate in any of that and call it good? Sadly, many do.

How do we transform and renew our mind? The same way we train to develop any other skill or way of thinking; We train our words, thoughts, and behaviors to match new ideals. As with any desire to change our lives, the first big step is to commit. Half-hearted measures never work in anything we do. One is 'all in' or one isn't in at all. We transform by leaving worldly ways behind forever. Don't be a fanatic, rather simply say "no" to old, worldly ways and invest your time, instead, in better life choices. Where your mind is concerned, "garbage in, garbage out." So, pump high quality, wonderful things into your head and avoid the garbage. Don't try to rush this. God's transforming work in you takes time. He wants your willing heart not an instantaneous perfect performance.

Focus on God in everything you do. Keep God always in your thoughts no matter what you're doing. Memorize verses of Scripture, meditate on them, and pray them often. Learning to put God first in all things manifests in your behavior, your speech, and is evident in your approach to all you do. Soon enough, this behavior develops a Christian worldview in you which dictates how you live every day. Your newly transformed mind permeates every part of your life. Transformed people live differently. They shed old worldly ways and adopt God's ways. They trade bad habits for great ones. They stop living a worldly life and begin a life of walking with God. This is how one learns what God's will for them is. Go for it!

"This is the day the Lord has made. Rejoice! And be glad in it." Smile - To make room for the new, the old has to get kicked to the curb. You can do this! You must! Now get out there and make this a Power Day.

Something to Ponder:

Champions are not judged by the number of times they fail, but by the number of times they succeed. **Anonymous**

Take a moment and give that quote some serious thought. Can you recall any time in your life when you have seen, heard or attended any awards ceremony where someone being honored for their various achievements had to stand quietly composed and listen as all their failures were made public for all to hear? Don't dwell on that too long. It never happens. What we hear about are all the honoree's accomplishments. We hear the respect, the glory, the accolades, the joys, and all things positive.

The well-known but always *unspoken* fact about champions is that their successes number much lower than the number of failures encountered on their way to achieving those successes. They didn't let failure stop them, though. They kept trying. Obviously, no-one ever succeeds if, when they experience failure, simply stop trying. Success results from a process of learning, trying, failing, learning more, adjusting, trying again, practicing all the time, not quitting, then failing some more and trying again....and again....and again. Ask any successful person.

The so-called "overnight sensation" is not really an "overnight" success. The reality is that "overnight" usually represents years of hard work, sacrifice, setbacks and overcoming failure to find success. Today's world would love for you believe that success comes so easily; that you're entitled to it and that the amount of effort required is minimal. Witness the myriad ads that claim, "no experience necessary. No inventory, no selling, no hard work, no effort, and it all happens so fast!!" If you think such things are true, please brace yourself. I'm about to make you mad because that notion is bogus. It's a myth - an outright lie. Consider this: How much would you willingly pay someone for a service or product knowing the person selling it has no experience and put forth no effort in that product or service? I'm guessing not much. Now that we've got that out of the way - you're now free to get busy. Take heart, Friend. It's the journey of hard work, paying the dues, conquering the challenges, and living your purpose that makes it a worthwhile adventure, anyway!

If success was easy, devoid of failure, came without challenge, it would be boring and routine. Everyone would be successful. Not everyone is successful – proof positive that the easy road is a myth. Let me encourage you to not get down simply because you run into a challenge or experience failure. Just know that challenges and even failures are road signs that will help you reach the success you're working for. And when you succeed, you'll know you earned it. And that's worth celebrating. Today, go get your success. Don't let anything stop you. God created you for His good purpose. Succeed in that!

"This is the day the Lord has made. Rejoice! And be glad in it." Smile - It's about your heart and the real trophy is God's smile. That's victory. Now get out there and make this a Power Day.

NOTES

Proverbs 20:30: "Lashes and wounds purge away evil, and beatings cleanse the innermost parts."

This Proverb, on the surface and out of context, sounds cruel and abusive, doesn't it? Without digging into it, many cultures practiced public floggings, telling their children they would get the "tar beat out of them," and other such foolishness. But, as always, there's more to this proverb and it is out of context, so we need to dig deeper to fully understand what is being said. There is an implied presumption here. Whatever any form of discipline might be, we presume it is applied appropriately, with love and wisdom. If it were not so, the discipline would be mere cruelty and cruelty teaches only wrong, harmful lessons. Another important point is this: punishment and discipline are *NOT* the same thing.

In this world, there are people who either just don't get it or who truly don't care. They never play by the rules, so to speak. It is one thing to be a bit rowdy, unruly and a bit wild. Being seriously out of line or even criminal is altogether different. Whether in a family, on the job, or in society, there are times when tougher discipline or harsher punishment is needed to gain a person's full attention so they can be helped to return to the path of wisdom and, hopefully, stay there. How far does your child have to go before reaching the last resort and warm the "foundation of his character" with a well-placed swat? At some point, the boss will tell the rebel employee, "Enough! You're fired!" How many long visits to the *Big House* will it take before the criminal finally understands he needs real life change? When the judge sentences him to life with no hope of parole? Lashes and wounds don't have to be physical in nature.

There are times we go to the doctor for help with an injury and find out a band aid isn't enough. Sometimes, the doctor must take extra measures to effect healing and those measures can be painful. A lot of operations happen every day to remove something from our bodies that either no longer work properly or never belonged in our body in the first place. Surgery can hurt. Broken bones won't heal properly if the doctor doesn't first set it back into its correct position. That hurts, but it gets the right results and there's no other way to accomplish those results. Bad teeth must be drilled on or extracted. Left alone, they will fester, and horrible things would happen. Likewise, there comes a time when words won't work, and action is demanded. I once saw a poster in favor of our 2nd Amendment rights that said, "When England tried to take guns away from Americans, Washington didn't *talk* to them....."

Important things occur daily in our nation and some politicians simply don't listen to their people. When the next election rolls around, they learn all about listening when they're voted out of office. At times, discipline must be painful to clarify important points and achieve proper behavior. No, I'm not talking about forced labor or coercion for immoral or illegal purposes. I'm talking about achieving good behavior.

It is so in our relationship with God. It is foolish to think we can disobey God's will as we wish and still expect life to be all blue skies and roses. He will warn, scold and try everything possible to get us to conform but at some point, if we continue to rebel, He will provide great clarity and chances are high that lesson will hurt – like when you got caught doing _____that one time. We know this is true. God is indeed a God of love. He is also just and He doesn't play favorites. Knowing that, wisdom dictates we avoid crossing the line in the first place. Today, as you walk, watch your step. If unsure, maybe try a new route.

"This is the day the Lord has made. Rejoice and be glad in it." Smile - When you wonder how far you can go, does it apply to what you can get away with or what you're capable of? Choose well. Now get out there and make this a Power Day.

Consider This:

"We look for solutions in many places, but where is the solution? It is in the human heart." **Anonymous**

It happens almost every day. Whether at work or home, in a family or with our friends, maybe from an unexpected source, a problem arises. When it does, it presents a question that demands an answer. Where do we turn?

We do our own research online. Perhaps, if warranted, we consult with experts. It's almost a given we will talk with trusted family and friends. Could be we'll read what others have said or done in similar sets of circumstances. To be sure, doing so does serve a purpose. However, when we think about it, that isn't where the answer will be found. That is where the advice and examples come from. What we need to remember is that all that advice pertains to problems that are similar and at best, very close, but will most likely not be exactly the same.

The answer we really need is found inside ourselves. Absolutely, it is good to know what she or he or they did when they faced a problem. But he, she and they are not going to solve our problem. That job falls to us. It falls to us to weigh the evidence, study the facts and, eventually, decide on the course of action we'll take. We use our imagination. We get creative. We might even become bold and try something different. What we really discover is what's been inside of us all along and the courage to bring it out.

The notions "We always do it this way" and "We've never done it that way before" can often be locks on the doorway to real progress and drain the potential for success. It is true that "If you always do what you've always done, you're always going to get what you've always gotten," and that is not the right answer. You need something new and different, so you have to do something new and different.

When you're faced with trying to solve a problem, you have a choice. You could see that what you and everyone else has done before isn't working and conclude it's an impossible problem. Or, you could ask, "What can I do differently?" and march into brand new territory and make an awesome discovery.

So that's it. Short, sweet, and to the point: Use your imagination and unlock the dormant parts of your life and go on an adventure. Try something different. It is highly probably the only thing keeping you in the rut is you. You can break free when you truly want to break free. Today is a new day. Do something new. Search your heart, find the real answer and solve the problem.

"This is the day the Lord has made. Rejoice! And be glad in it." Smile - Oh yeah…"new" takes faith and confidence and God. Now get out there and make this a Power Day.

Something to Ponder:

"Love is an irresistible desire to be irresistibly desired." **Robert Frost**.

I intend no disrespect to Mr. Frost but my initial impression of his words in this statement raised several red flags immediately in my mind. First, his definition of love could be misleading because it compels us to think love, for everyone, is selfish. Second, his definition of love is spot on for many because people have an amazing capacity for selfishness and those who are [selfish] are lost as to what love really is. Third, anyone with any real-life experience at all will tell you that being irresistibly desired can get very tedious really fast. Not to mention the potential to make the person desiring you seem clingy, obsequious, and just plain creepy.

When it comes to my own irresistibility, my wife would quickly point out, lovingly, of course and in an effort to help me maintain a healthy level of humility - "Jeff, trust me, that won't be a problem for you." True, but part of me wants to be *a little* irresistible. It's not necessarily bad to want to be desirable...but when *that* desire to be desired becomes the essence of love in our minds and grows into an irresistible desire...we've crossed a line into something that doesn't resemble love at all. The desire to be irresistibly desired can lead a person to do some unhealthy things to become whatever they envision as "irresistibly desirable." That can be destructive, make someone manipulative and narcissistic. Pretty sure that is not what God had in mind for us when He talked about love.

God is love. God is a giver. God's love is unconditional. His love is free. His love is always available. The love God demonstrates for us is never selfish in any manner. We don't have to do anything for Him to make Him love us. His love gives, it serves, it protects, it's humble, and it expects nothing in return. God's desire is to see those He loves happy, safe, fulfilled, and whole. God's love isn't about Him, it's about those He loves.

God loved you so much He sacrificed His own Son as atonement for your sin. I don't care where you come from, that's a big deal! If God's desire is to be irresistibly desired, do you think He would have done that knowing that so many would look at that incredible sacrifice and turn their backs on it? No! When people turn away....it's not really irresistible, is it?

So, today, my Friends, love is not about being irresistibly desired. It's about having the irresistible desire to serve and love others. It's knowing the sacrifice you make for someone else is far more important than your own personal comfort. Love is not weak....it is powerful. Love is not timid...it is courageous. Love is not yours to keep or manipulate or control....it's yours to give so others can be better. Today....love others the way God loves you.

"This is the day the Lord has made. Rejoice! And be glad in it." Smile - 'Nuff said? Now get out there and make this a Power Day.

Proverbs 7: 1-4: "My son, obey my words, and treasure my commands. Keep my commands and live; protect my teachings as you would the pupil of your eye. Tie them to your fingers; write them on the tablet of your heart. Say to wisdom, 'You are my sister,' and call understanding your relative."

My wife and I were fans of the reality show, "The Biggest Loser" for a while because one of the contestants, who went on to win the big prize, Danny Cahill, lives in our city. The irony of the show, if you will, is that the people who participated in that series were all winners...who lost. They lost weight… lots and lots of weight. More importantly, they lost fear. They lost the will to be sad. They lost doubt and they lost stress. They lost anxiety about themselves and they lost apprehension in the world around them.

While only one person won the big bucks at the end, they all came away winners. They won the new, healthier body they worked so hard for. ("the old is gone, the new is come...." 2 Cor. 5:17) They won confidence. Some won it for the first time and others won it back. ("I can do all things...through Christ." Phil. 4:13) They won self-esteem.("...because I am fearfully and wonderfully made." Pslm.139:14) They won love from each other, from family and friends but most of all; they won by learning to love themselves. ("And the second great command, love your neighbor as yourself." Mth 19:19)

They didn't have to get there all by themselves. They had friends cheering for them. They had coaches and mentors to guide and instruct them. Motivation came from sources the contestants were previously unaware of and there was someone who never gave up on them. They won all these things. No one handed them a freebie and said, 'Here's your new body and a new attitude... just go put it on." Someone simply said to them, "I care. I can help. W-O-R-K with me!" They accepted the help and did what they were told. They struggled through the tough workouts, the challenges, the doubts and fears, the pain, the setbacks, the disappointments....and they didn't quit. Each little victory spurred them on to the next little victory and in the end, all those little victories culminated in winning the war. ("Let us not become weary in doing good, for at the proper time, we will reap a harvest if we do not give up." Gal. 6:9)

That process described is much like our Christian walk. It applies to every facet of our lives through obedience, keeping His commands, treasuring the Word, doing the work, and struggling through by focusing on the goal. What we focus on is what gets into our heads, which has a direct affect our thinking, which in turn creates new habits and ultimately builds our character. No one ever told the contestants on "The Biggest Loser" that it would be easy. They only told them it would be worth it. And it was. It still is. God never said our walk would be easy - only worth it. It only takes a decision to be a Christian, but it takes guts, determination, effort, and a lot a courage to walk that life. But it's worth it and our success is found in doing what God tells us in His word: obey, treasure His commands, protect in your heart what God has taught you, keep His word tied to you, seek wisdom and understanding and live it boldly.

"This is the day the Lord has made. Rejoice! And be glad in it." Smile - Stick with God. He'll make you 'The Biggest Winner." Now get out there and make this a Power Day.

Something to Ponder:

"Healing doesn't mean the damage never existed. It means the damage no longer controls our lives." Anonymous

If you've attended church, small groups, Sunday school classes or any gathering where Christians meet to talk about life, the Bible, God, and how it all fits together, it is likely you've heard stories from people that sound like: "I used to be _____(fill the blank with any issue) but Jesus came into my life and I'm not like that anymore." The issues run the gamut of drugs, alcohol abuse, regrettable behaviors or issues with depression, spousal abuse, anger, fear, and on and on. You may have heard them. We all have a story of what we used to be and now we're not.

While it may sound cliché, it is true that churches are not playhouses for hypocrites and Holier-than-thou types but rather, they are "hospitals" for sinners. Just as a rehab center is not a social club for celebrities who faced serious challenges in their lives, they are hospitals where people who are thoroughly messed up can find the help they really need. In either case, reality dictates there is always some rate of recidivism. The world calls it "falling off the wagon." Christians call it backsliding. It's when we revert to the old ways.

Falling off the wagon happens because once a person is addicted to something, their ability to make good and wise choices is severely affected. Can they become an ex-addict? Yes, but it's a daily choice. I'm an ex-smoker who used to drink a lot! I smoked almost two packs a day. I finally decided to quit smoking "cold turkey" on September 1, 1988. I quit drinking because it made me want a cigarette. All these years later, I am still always one drag on a cigarette away from that same habit even though I've not been anywhere near a cigarette in decades. An alcoholic is always one sip...not a drink...a sip away from falling off the wagon. Conquering an addiction is a daily task that never ends. It gets easier with practice. Attitudes change, behaviors improve but one can never let one's guard down.

The healing was effective. Damage, however, leaves scars. We're healthy again but we carry a forever reminder to make good choices. We Christians are in the world - not of it - but we live *in* the world. The world can't leave town so keeping the sin monkey off our backs and avoiding more damage is a daily thing. Temptation is always a threat. That's why it's very important to exercise your faith and strengthen your belief. Attending church regularly is vital; prayer needs to be a daily regimen. It's why mentors, accountability partners, small groups, and just plain fellowship are all critical elements in the Christian life. We can't heal on our own.

None of us broke away from the 'old man' all by ourselves and none of us can stay away from him by ourselves. It is one thing to "be transformed by the renewing of you mind..." It's a whole 'nother thing to stay that way. See, the enemy continues "prowling around like a lion looking for someone to devour." The AA organization has an army of people whose purpose is to stay connected with members to keep them on track. How often does someone call you - or how often do you reach out to your friends and ask them how their walk is going? Jesus took care of the healing part. Our part is to guard our hearts and remain in Him.

"This is the day the Lord has made. Rejoice and be glad in it." Smile – Rejoice in the healing. Now get out there and make this a Power Day.

NOTES

Something To Ponder:

2 Chronicles 7:14: "...if My people who are called by My name humble themselves, pray and seek My face, and turn from their evil ways, then I will hear from heaven, forgive their sin, and heal their land."

It's important to know and understand that this verse is a general rule that can have broad application so we must be careful not to force it into specific situations where it may not fit. By that, I mean it is true that sin and turning away from God always results in trouble. But not all trouble is a result of sin. Remember that in determining the validity of applying any biblical rule or principle; you should be able to reinforce it with other Biblical Scriptures. If you can't do that, you may need to rethink your position.

Notice also this promise is conditioned on a set of actions from us. "**If** My people _humble_ themselves and _pray -_ and _seek-_ and _turn from evil - THEN_, I will...." Sound familiar? "If" is the set of conditions that must be met to prompt God to act. Just as sin results in trouble, sincere repentance, true humility, honestly seeking God's face and shunning evil results in forgiveness, healing, restoration, and new life. What happens if the conditions are not met? A few verses later, V. 19 forward, God lays down the law and warns Solomon of rejection, plagues, ridicule, droughts, and more if Israel strays away from Him to worship other gods. "If you....I will." If you don't....woe betide you. And God isn't joking.

Let me say this and you examine your own life to see if I'm right. How well or how poorly your life is going can be directly traced back to one thing: the status of your personal relationship with God. **Galatians 6:7**....."a man reaps what he sows." If you've sown good seed, your crops should be good. If you've sown bad seed, things will not be so rosy. But God says, "If you....turn, pray, humble, seek....I will forgive and heal."

Here's a "Captain Obvious" moment. If you stick your finger in the flame on the stove, your nerves immediately call your brain and cry, "Help!" Your brain instantly replies with, "Take your finger out of the fire!" All the body parts involved in that process get the same message and you snap your hand back, yelp in pain, and grab something (butter, maybe) and jam your finger into it so it will stop hurting. All of that takes a fraction of a second. Then your body naturally begins to heal itself. Your brain registers a great lesson: "DO NOT DO THAT AGAIN....IT HURTS!" Now you're humble because you learned you're not impervious to pain by fire. You seek healing and acknowledge that it came from God! Then wisdom settles in and you apply the lesson learned by willingly and joyfully turning away from it.

And yet, we still sin, even though we know it's going to hurt and make us feel miserable. The lesson is there but we either "forget" or we just don't get it. Worst case, we're not really the Believer we think we are. God, like the good father He is, is saying, "If you'll just listen to me and do what I told you, you'll be fine. But, hey, it's your call." Today, examine your life to see what's what. Ask yourself and God, how's our relationship doing? Maybe you're the one who needs to make some changes. Maybe it's something that's just in the way and you need God's help. Either way, the answer is the same. Humble yourself. Pray. Seek out God. Repent. Do that and He will keep His promise to heal, forgive, restore, and make you whole. There's your first step. The most vital and important key is: You have to take that step first.

"This is the day the Lord has made. Rejoice and be glad in it." Smile - The good, new life is there, waiting. But we must let go of the old to get it. Now get out there and make this a Power Day.

Luke 23:43: "Jesus answered him, 'I tell you the truth, today you will be with me in paradise.'"

There were two thieves crucified with Jesus that day. One taunted the Savior. "Save yourself...and us!" What he really meant was, "Forget them...save _me_.... Get _me_ down from here!!" The other defended Christ's honor. It was he who recognized Who was next to him. It was he who asked God to enter his heart. It was to this thief that Jesus spoke His promise to save. That's really all we know from the Bible about these two men. They were thieves, sinners, caught, tried, convicted and sentenced to die in a horrible manner and presumably forgotten. Surely, there must be more to their story!

Think! Is this not to some extent, part of the story of all mankind? These men were likely common, everyday people trying to get along in this life. Perhaps survival was the focal reason for their actions. One took the path of crime perhaps because he had no heart and didn't care. He was selfish, out to get what he considered 'his' and to have it his way. Maybe he regarded those he hurt in the process as mere steppingstones in his path. Color him arrogant, angry, selfish, cruel, hardhearted, and un-caring.

The other may have taken that path out of desperation. He had no other choice. He had to survive. He didn't want to steal and he certainly never intended to hurt anyone. Hunger, neglect, fear, being unloved can drive one to do...to survive. He had to eat. If only there was a better way! All he had really wanted was just a chance. It never came until finally, in a hard and terrible place he discovered that better way and approached. Contact was made, an invitation sent, received and accepted. This one goes from begging crumbs to occupying a seat at the finest table imaginable.

Too often we find ourselves at the ends of our rope. Hope has all but vanished. It seems there's no way out. Life has been hard. We got through it our way - the only way we knew - until the day came our way didn't work and we were faced with a choice. Some people are so consumed with anger, resentment, and the bitterness of hard living they will reject the one thing that can save them. Some recognize that last glimmer of hope and with their last ounce of courage reach to grab hold of it. Some accept the invite. Others reject it. Those who accept the invitation come to know peace and joy in their hearts from knowing once and for all what it is to have hope fulfilled and experience the amazing love of God.

Maybe you have already had your day when you found yourself in that frightful place and you made a choice. You chose Jesus. Maybe you're wondering what to do because that is the choice you're facing. Choose life! God is 'the way, the truth, and the life.' He is the One who came to give you life in abundance, with a purpose, with hope and an incredible future. Choose life! "All who believe in Him shall have eternal life." Choose life! That's your choice today. It is the most important choice you will ever make. "This day I call heaven and earth as witnesses against you that I have set before you life and death, blessings and curses. Now choose life, so that you and your children may live and that you may love the Lord your God, listen to His voice, and hold fast to Him." **Deuteronomy 30: 19-20**

God created you. He lived for you and set an example. He took upon Himself all your sins and paid the price in full with His own blood. You are free! All you need to do is choose. Choose life!

"This is the day the Lord has made. Rejoice and be glad in it." Smile - Sin is forgiven. Death is conquered. Jesus loves you. Choose life! Now get out there and make this a Power Day.

Psalm 71:1-2: "Lord, I seek refuge in You; never let me be disgraced. In Your justice, rescue and deliver me; listen closely to me and save me.

Acts 4:12: "There is salvation in no one else, for there is no other name under heaven given to people by which we must be saved."

God is a saver....a savior, but not just any savior...He is *the* Savior. He likes to save His people and make sure they are safe from the attacks of the enemy. He doesn't just save your soul for life eternal.

I like to think God gets a good bit of satisfaction any time Satan gets robbed of souls and Heaven's population grows. He's saves by being our refuge - a place to find protection, relief from stress. God rescues and delivers us. He is the One who alone can heal our soul, mend our spirit, and restore us to His own heart.

Notice that the psalmist actively sought out the Lord as One in Whom he could find that kind of solace and comfort. He sought God first because he knew in his heart the only place to find real protection was God. That isn't something we could ever hope to do by ourselves. Man is able to help to an extent, but man cannot deliver us from the attacks of our common enemy. Only God can do that.

Where do you go when you're stressed? What do you do to find relief and comfort and peace? Are you one to immediately ask God..."In this situation I'm going through, please don't let me disgrace myself or You."? All too often we humans look first at the situation we're in and it frightens us. We become more fearful instead of turning first to God. That fear makes us forget what is truly important - like God and HIs promises – so we end up putting ourselves through a lot of unnecessary pain and heartache and frustration. If we would simply remember that we are God's people and that He loves us, we could bypass all that fear and the negative stuff would diminish greatly.

No, life's trials won't just disappear, and we still have to walk through our challenges, but we can find rest for our souls, keep a clear head, maintain our joy and live wisely if we simply remember God and His word. His promises are there - active and available. We access those promises by faith. Inside the refuge that is Christ Jesus is where we find courage, endurance, strength, wisdom, humility, and everything we need to victoriously live the life God gave us. Turn to Him first for anything and everything and know God saves where no one and nothing else can. He is your refuge – your Savior.

"This is the day the Lord has made. Rejoice and be glad in it." Smile - When playing hide-n-seek with life's troubles, God's refuge is an absolute win. Now get out there and make this a Power Day.

Proverbs 12:4a: "A wife of noble character is her husband's crown..."

Proverbs 31:10 "A wife of noble character who can find? She is worth far more than rubies."

Look at two important things defining a wife of noble character. First, she is a true asset to her husband. She is the reason he gets noticed at all. She is his crown. Consider: if you're wearing a crown and walk into a room full of people, they *will* notice it right away. Yes, a husband is the spiritual head of a family by God's design but know that a crown's place is *ON TOP* of the head. Secondly, she is rare ("who can find...) and because she's rare, she possesses great worth. Okay, that's great and all but what's the point? Simply this: are you treating your wife the way God wants you to?

God says your wife, my wife, is a very special person and she is of immense value to Him. He went to a lot of time and effort to create that woman just for you. She isn't just any woman. God custom designed her to be your perfect match. Gents, our wives literally are God's gift to us. Ladies, if your husband asks, "What you think you are, God's gift?" you would be correct and truthful in saying, "Yes. Why? Did you forget?"

Ladies, though it is sometimes misunderstood, please know that Proverbs 31 does not limit you nor does it make outrageous demands on you. Rather, it opens the door to a host of possibilities. No one can be, or do, all the things listed in this Proverb, but it certainly gives any woman options to fulfilling her own purpose. We would all be wise to note that the commonality throughout verses 10 to the end of this Proverb is that a wife of noble character brings wisdom into the tapestry that is her life and the life of her family. A wife of noble character is a huge deal.

So, Men! What are you doing to make sure your crown – this gift from God who's responsible for making sure you get the respect you deserve - shines as she deserves? How do we do that? We make sure the home she lives in - "her home" - is paid for, safe, secure and in good repair. We work and sacrifice as necessary to provide for her and our children. We ensure the kids fully understand that (a) we don't disrespect God and (b) we never, ever disrespect momma. Men, in my humble opinion there is absolutely no excuse under God's heaven for any child to ever bad mouth, disobey, or disrespect his/her mother. Don't forget: Long before she was that child's mom, she was your wife. Long before she was your gift from God, she was His child, and it should be burned on your heart that NO BODY – including her children - disrespects your wife. She's your crown! How she is treated is on you, Husband.

You can help your crown gleam brightly by ensuring that next to the love of God, she feels safest with you. Your wife should never be afraid of you, at all, ever. Let me be very bold and very clear here. We are to protect our wives and it is _**never**_ okay to "slap her around a little." Men who do that are a whole list of words and phrases I am not allowed to even think, much less say. Cowards hit women. Losers abuse women. It is criminal; it's disgusting; it is weak; it is shameful. 'Nuff said?

Help her around the house. It won't kill you to pick up after yourself and set a good example for the kids who are not to disrespect mama. Our wives are not our servants. They are our wives. God's gift to us. We love them and in loving them, we do not use them. We serve them. No, that doesn't mean they don't have to do anything and shirk their own responsibilities. It just means that we can help. If we don't take good care of our crown, we're disrespecting God's daughter. Make her feel valued by letting her know she is important to you. Listen to her. Pay attention. Sacrifice self. Do that sort of thing and she will be your crown. She will shine and you will be the guy who wears that crown. When you treat your crown with love, dignity and honor, you get treated like a king and ...say it with me, Guys...."It is good to be the king."

"This is the day the Lord has made. Rejoice! And be glad in it." Smile - "Happy wife, happy life." Now get out there and make this a Power Day.

Something to Ponder:

"That you may retain your self-respect, it is better to displease the people by doing what you know is right, than to temporarily please them by doing what you know is wrong." **William J. H. Boetcker**

Whatever your personal walk in life might be, you will always have ample opportunity to make decisions or statements and take actions guaranteed to upset other people. Parents and politicians, CEO's, judges, talk radio hosts, and drivers in traffic to name but a few do this every day.

Parents the world over know it is right for children to be in school. They also know there are times when the "tummy ache" the child claims to have really means, "I have a test today and I'm not ready." Mom now has a choice to make: Displease my child and make him go to school or please him and let him stay home. Doing the right thing will not make her popular but doing the wrong thing plants wrong ideas in the child's mind. What to do? Any good parent does what is right knowing the child will learn something of value from the experience. "You're fine. Have a great day in class!"

Of course, leadership never makes you *Numero Uno* on everyone's "Favorite People" list, but people will respect you. Fact of life: If you respect yourself, others will also respect you. If you don't, neither will they. "And the second is like unto it, Love your neighbor as yourself." **(Mth 22:39)** Self-respect. Jesus made it a high priority; love God and love others like you love yourself! It is Number Two on God's list of the most important things we must do. He repeats it often in the Bible. One great result of having a healthy self-respect is that it makes it easier to do what is right instead of worrying about others may think.

You have integrity and honor. You do nothing out of malice or spite. You do right only because it's the right thing to do. The Bible says that "whatever your hand finds to do, do it as unto the Lord and not unto man." Pop Quiz! Whose opinion counts? God's, not man's. Maybe you're thinking, "Oh sure, tell that to my boss. He thinks his opinion is pretty important." Friend, if you are working as unto the Lord, wishing to please Him, your work will reflect the quality and skill God gave you to live your purpose. You will do well - not for your earthly boss - but for your Heavenly Father and your earthly boss will notice.

Self-respect says to us Christians, "I am a child of God who created me with skill, ability, dreams, and the free will to be the best I can be for His glory. I can do - and so I shall." Fear of what man thinks or being afraid that doing right will somehow end badly for you are excuses. I can promise that doing what is right won't always be easy or without significant challenge, but it will be right, and it will eventually end well and in God's favor. Let me encourage you today to do the right thing regardless of what others think. Ignore the enemy's lies. Stand firm in your faith and know God's promises are real and effective. You'll be very glad you did. Self-respect: love yourself and others will love you, too. God loves you!

"This is the day the Lord has made. Rejoice! And be glad in it." Smile - God Almighty took the time to create you! That makes you special! Now get out there and make this a Power Day.

NOTES

Proverbs 2: 7-8: "He stores up success for the upright; He is a shield for those who live with integrity so that He may guard the paths of justice and protect the way of His loyal followers."

I hope we can agree that what God wants from us, and what we need with Him, is relationship. Good, you're nodding in agreement. Can we also agree that everyone involved in any good relationship gives and receives from each other in terms of time, effort, listening, actions, understanding, patience, and so on? Wonderful, we're off to a good start. Since we can agree on those two things: we want and need relationship with God and in that relationship, giving and receiving takes place on both sides, then it's easy to see why many of His promises to us begin with the words, "If you..." followed shortly thereafter by the words, "then I will..." If you do this, then I will do that. It's not a bribe. It's not a trick. It's a relationship in which, in every case, when everyone does their part, everyone benefits.

Open your bibles and look at the verses in Proverbs 2 leading up to verse 7. What we find are several of these conditions: (and sometimes, the "if you..." is implied or understood) "If you....accept my words;....listen closely to wisdom....; if you direct your heart to understanding...; if you seek....if you call out to insight...." THEN....what? "You will understand the fear of the Lord...; discover the knowledge of God...;" and ...on into the passage above.

Our part in this relationship *is not* to wake up in the morning and over our first cup of coffee give God instructions on how we're His kids, that He owes us and how it's time for Him to shower us with blessing and success. If that was your idea up to now, it's time to abandon that wrong idea and head in the right direction. God is _not_ our personal Santa Clause who meets our every demand and satisfies our every whim. The truth is this is how it should go: You and I, willingly and with a great attitude, joy in our hearts, and dogged determination, seek after God's wisdom for us. We soak it up and make sure we've done absolutely everything we must and can do to understand God's will and word and we strive to live it daily. *THEN,* (then as in after) having done our part, God has the freedom to do His. His part - _IF_ you've done yours - is storing up success (resourcefulness), shielding you while those who didn't do their part are under attack. He guards you on the path to justice and protects those loyal to Him. Success, shielding, protection, guarding.

Kindly note: He did not say all the obstacles would be cleared away. He never mentioned how easy, if at all, it was going to be. All He said was that you, because of your diligence and willingness to seek Him, would be protected, guarded, shielded, and find success. That could take some time. It may come with challenges and some of those might be tough. But, if you...then God will. That's how we tap into His promises and find His blessing and favor. It's not about works! It is just us doing our part in a true relationship.

Do you get that? It's important because as soon as you're done reading this, there will be a quiz and it will take us all day to complete that quiz. Seek Him. Go after His will and work to understand it. By doing so, you gain wisdom and knowledge and then you find success. Today, do what it takes to find success in God and then, you'll gain even more understanding! How great it is that?!

"This is the day the Lord has made. Rejoice! And be glad in it." Smile - "Seek Him first...All things shall be added." If you, then He will. Now get out there and make this a Power Day.

Something to Ponder:

"To win one hundred victories in one hundred battles is not the highest skill. To subdue the enemy without fighting is the highest skill." **Ginchin Funakoshi**

In order to both win a battle and avoid peril during that battle, a warrior must know two things well. He must know his enemy and himself. If he has mastered the knowledge of both, he will always avoid peril. Surprisingly, a lot more people should be able to claim that mastery. If you know yourself well but little of your enemy, your best hope is to come out even. If you don't know either one very well, it will not go well for you on the battlefield. If you're honest with yourself, knowing you should be easy. The question is, "How can I possibly know enough about all my enemies?" The answer is simple: You don't have enemies. You have one enemy. That one, however, is a master of disguises and the father of lies. He wants you to think our enemies are other people or the various circumstances impacting our lives. Regardless of the disguise or circumstance, it's always the same enemy. If you learn to recognize that enemy and are sure you know who and what you are in Christ, victory is assured before any conflict happens.

Notice! This is key! I did NOT say victory is *yours*. I said victory is *assured*. For Christians, the battle always belongs to the Lord. Knowing that is part of knowing yourself and who you are in Christ. Sure, a guy can be a great technical "fighter" on the daily battlefields of life. He can beat people up with facts, figures and even Scripture while destroying others with a harsh tongue. That's not a good or enviable skill. That's being a bully and the type of Christian that gives Christians a bad rep. Other than chasing the moneychangers out of the temple, can you recall a single time when Jesus got physically violent with anyone to win a battle? No. He didn't have to. He always won using words, love, compassion, and positive actions. He was never weak. He was never cowardly, nor did He ever allow anyone to intimidate Him. But He "subdued the enemy without fighting." Every time.

We can do likewise. It won't always be easy or quick, but it always works. How do I win without fighting? The enemy has one agenda: break you down and get you to abandon your faith. God gave you that faith. Jesus already overcame death and the devil. You know that, so: Hold on to your faith. Trust God's word and His promises. Know that victory is already assured and that you are a child of the Most High God. This is a God who takes care of His own and has promised you can "resist the devil and he will flee far from you." Don't cave into fear. Stop worrying. Do not allow doubt to throw you off track. When confusion comes, remember that's the enemy attacking so stop, think, get back on track and keep going. Return good for evil. Say 'no' to that which deserves a 'no' and 'yes' to what you know is right and good. Friend, no one can force you to be anything other than what God intended you to be unless you allow it. Don't allow it. You are not stuck in any situation. With Christ in you, you can stand up under anything and come out on top. You already have the ability to exhibit the highest skill in every battle and subdue the enemy without ever physically fighting. Use it.

"This is the day the Lord has made, Rejoice! And be glad in it." Smile - To win without fighting you must stay very calm. Now get out there and make this a Power Day.

Psalm 27: 1: "The Lord is my light and my salvation - whom shall I fear? The Lord is the stronghold of my life - of whom should I be afraid?"

David trusted God. He referred often to God as his refuge, his stronghold, and his shield. David truly and rightly believed in his heart that he had nothing to fear from anything or anyone because God is a God who protects and keeps His word. For David, that's all there was to it. Even in his human failings, David never let go of his faith or allowed his beliefs to weaken. He was never afraid. David had relationship.

In the USA, on March 23, 2010, history was made. That day, the Affordable Care Act, known commonly as "Obamacare," became law. Many believed, and actual experience proved they were right, that this history making law was not remotely helpful or anything close to an improvement. At the time, there were many questions and doubts. People were fearful of losing access to good, quality medical care. They were more fearful of being subjected to an oppressive, totalitarian government to any degree and the loss of more freedoms and liberties for the sake of false promises. To a great degree, they were right. The ACA was, and remains, bad law. There were more restrictions on our freedoms and liberties. Time corrected parts of that showing the fears were valid but instead of giving them to the One who could assuage them, those fears were misplaced.

In times of trouble, worry, and crisis, it is easy to fall into fear. If you are fearful or worried, please hear this: God is your source. He is our only source. Yes, we have a duty to be good citizens and stand for what is true, right, and good. We should always do that. But President Obama is likely still of the belief he stated publicly that "government is the answer to everything." He is grossly mistaken. In truth, this government, or any government, is rarely the correct answer to anything. Actual results proved that despite this new healthcare law, government could not heal us or even properly administer an individual health plan. The misguided idea that bigger government is more able to supply our needs, falls victim to the massive amounts of proof that say otherwise.

God provides immeasurably more than all we need. Government cannot live your life for you and those running it are not nearly smart nor capable enough to correctly dictate how you should live. God, however, has proven Himself to be an expert guide for all areas of our life. Government cannot properly or lovingly raise your children, but God's word contains every we need to be good and loving parents, without fail. There is much the government finds impossible to do. "With God, all things are possible." Governments threaten, coerce, and demand. God loves, gives, and encourages. Governments made by man are doomed to fail or fall or be corrupt. God cannot be corrupted and He stands forever. Even with their best efforts, governments and governors struggle to keep a promise or their word. God has kept every promise He ever made. His word is trustworthy and reliable.

Today, be one who trusts God and finds all your resources and confidence in Him. Stand for what is true. Fight for what is right. Be loyal to the real Constitution and your nation. Strive to be civil and law-abiding always, even in protest. Remember, God protects; God supplies; God guides; God imparts wisdom; God is our refuge and our source for all things! Knowing that, we have nothing and no-one to fear.

"This is the day the Lord has made. Rejoice and be glad in it." Smile - Be strong. Be courageous. God is with you. Now get out there and this a Power Day.

Something to Ponder:

"Challenges, when faced with confidence and strength, will transform you."
Jeffrey D. Hill

Well, when you put it *that* way.... Rising to meet a challenge sounds like a noble, wise, and courageous thing to do and something that builds our character. That's because that is what it is! When facing any challenge, the most important thing we discover is who we really are. We discover our own character. It may not seem like it at the time but that's a good thing. If we didn't meet at least some resistance along life's path, there are many important aspects of our own nature we would never know.

Here is another way God says it: "Therefore, since we have been justified through faith, we have peace with God through our Lord Jesus Christ, through Whom we have gained access by faith into the hope of the glory of God. Not only so, but *we also rejoice in our sufferings, because we know that suffering produces perseverance; perseverance, character; and character, hope.* And hope does not disappoint us, because God has poured out His love into our hearts by the Holy Spirit, whom He has given us." **Romans 5: 1-5** (emphasis mine)

Rejoice in our sufferings. Rejoice means to be glad about something. The thesaurus uses a lot of words to describe suffering and none of them *sounded* like anything to be very glad about. So why is God asking us to rejoice in our sufferings? He said it's because "suffering produces perseverance." As they say, "what doesn't kill you, only makes you stronger." The stronger we are (the more we persevere) the more our character is enhanced. We become wiser. We're able to endure more. We make better decisions and that makes us better people. Persevering people have hope and hopeful people live better lives. "Hope does not disappoint." Now, would you agree that is something to rejoice over?

The opposite of disappointment is satisfaction. Hope satisfies. Challenges help us discover who we are. A lot of folks are paralyzed by challenges. Occasionally, some of those folks are you and me. Instead of becoming paralyzed, we can deliberately persevere, powered by hope. There are lots of people suffering greatly who could, if they wished, sit around feeling sorry for themselves, discouraged by what they face every day. In fact, most won't do that. Nor do they merely do just enough to get by. Hopeful people actively live life, constantly testing the limits of their ability. They persevere. They are people of character. They have hearts filled with hope and they treat life's challenges as a gift. So, what challenges are you facing? What will you do about them? It's your choice.

"This is the day the Lord has made. Rejoice! And be glad in it." Smile - Perseverance builds character. Character creates hope. Hope allows us to really live. Now get out there and make this a Power Day.

1 Corinthians 10: 12-13: "So, if you think you are standing firm, be careful that you don't fall! No temptation has seized you except what is common to man. And God is faithful; He will not let you be tempted beyond what you can bear. But when you are tempted, He will also provide a way out so that you can stand up under it."

Mother Theresa was an amazing individual who set a marvelous example of what it means to share the love, the grace, the mercy, and the hope of God to the world. Because she did so, the devil would have hated what she did and, no doubt, presented her with myriad temptations. Temptation comes along daily. According to God's word, none of it is new or any big surprise to God or us, for that matter. He is certainly not caught off guard. It is safe to say none of us will ever hear God say, "Whoa! I did **not** see that coming!"

It seems like most of the time when we hear the word *temptation,* we more often think of things like lying, stealing, envy, greed, or something of a lusty nature. Those are, indeed, common to all mankind. But then, we're also tempted by other sins that are equally common. Such things as fear, worry, doubt, laziness, and procrastination. What? Worry and doubt are sins? They can be in that they indicate a lack of trust in God and his ability to do all things. In case you were unaware, it's also sinful to neglect that which you know you're supposed to do. Those are sins of omission. Sins of commission and sins of omission both come with their own powerful tempters.

Some say all sins are the same in God's eyes. Yes, and no. When it comes to salvation and eternal consequences, all sins are against an eternal and infinite God and therefore all sins are subject to eternal consequence. **(Romans 6:23)** In that way, in God's eyes, all sin is the same in terms of penalty and in terms of forgivability, but not in terms of severity. It would be incorrect to say jaywalking and murder are on the same level. Some sins are worse than others. In Matthew 5:21-28, Jesus compares adultery to murder but that doesn't make them equal. His point there is to show that what we think in our minds is just as important as what we do. It was His original "Don't even think about it!" statement. We must guard our hearts AND minds AND actions! Kindly note this passage doesn't say "*if* you are tempted...' It says, "But *when* you are tempted..." We know it's coming – so we can be prepared for it. That's what practicing our spiritual discipline is for – equipping ourselves so we can resist the devil, honor God and properly guard our hearts and minds in Christ Jesus.

We have two things going for us and I think the key to success is simply to remember that we have them. All too often, we forget that there is no sin so big God cannot forgive. One, God won't let us be tempted by anything we can't handle. Sorry to burst this bubble but there's no question or excuse..."I just can't bear this!" Yes, you can! God has already given you the tools needed to do so. Two, there is a way out from under whatever is tempting or tormenting us. No need to wonder *IF* there is a way out because we already know that way exists. We need not fret about being crushed by that thing because "you can stand up under it." We must remember that key and *USE IT to find the way.* Believe that the word of Christ is true and His promises work in our favor. We will be faced with stuff. It isn't new -it's common. We know we can have victory over it. We have the God-given ability to handle it and there is a way out, courtesy of God Almighty. Today when temptations come - remember.

"This is the day the Lord has made. Rejoice! And be glad in it." Smile - In other words, stand up. Be committed. Hold fast. Now get out there and make this a Power Day!

NOTES

James 2:17 - 18: "In the same way faith, if it doesn't have works, is dead by itself. But someone will say, 'You have faith, and I have works.' Show me your faith without works, and I will show you my faith from my works."

When you read James, you realize quickly he was outspoken. After all, he's the half-brother of Jesus Christ so being honest and very upfront was just how he rolled. He actually said faith without works was dead. Faith had to be - and indeed must be - more than just words. What James said is true and allow me to also make exceedingly clear the vitally important point that we are saved *FOR* good works, *NOT BY* good works. If you're working to get saved, stop now. All such efforts are futile. We are saved by grace through faith, not by works. It's a gift. (**Ephesians 2:8-9**)

That being the case, it would do all of us some good if we periodically do a personal review to ensure we understand the difference between *saying* we're Christian and *being* Christian. That's what James was saying to people. It's one thing to claim Christianity but it's a whole other thing to actually live it. For instance: Why do you go to church every Sunday? Are you there to make sure the right folks see you and acknowledge your presence, or are you there for real fellowship and to learn how your brothers and sisters in Christ really are doing and how you might serve them? Are you at church for a quick pump-up from an inspiring spiritual thought or are you seeking God's truth you can apply to your life and effect lasting, meaningful growth in Christ? Are you looking for a convenient, user-friendly sermonette or searching for life-changing conviction from the authoritative power of "thus saith the Lord!"? Attending church for the right reasons is a work that builds, strengthens and empowers your faith.

Apply that same idea to every area of life. God is calling all of us to put feet to our faith and live as Christians. He doesn't need anyone to claim to be one, talk the talk and then live like a heathen the rest of the time. Living out what we claim to believe through our behavior at work or at home or in the grocery store or on the playing field is a great indicator of the validity of your words.

God's word tells us that the second most important thing we must do is to "love our neighbor as ourselves." Other drivers, co-workers and your fellow citizens are your neighbors. God tells us to return good for evil. Do you strive to say respectful things about someone who just insulted you or are you more ready to verbally tear him up? Are you ready to serve anywhere, anytime for anyone or more ready to say, "Oh Pastor, thanks for asking but I….well, I just can't……"? Do your works prove or betray your words?

My heart for you today is simply this: What are you doing in your life today to make sure that your walk and your talk are saying the same thing? That you're not just playing "church" but living a life that truly honors God by keeping His commands, respecting others, honoring authority, and loving people. Of course, it isn't easy. If it was, everyone would be Christian. If you really want to do a good work today and need something that will give you a challenge….live like a Christian.

"This is the day the Lord has made. Rejoice! And be glad in it." Smile - What if God loved us the same way we love Him? Makes you glad God's ways are higher than ours, huh? Now get out there and make this a Power Day.

Proverbs 21:5: "The plans of the diligent certainly lead to profit, but anyone who is reckless only becomes poor."

"Diligent," in this case, does not mean to hurry or to work quickly, even though diligent people tend to make the most of their time to get a job done well and in a timely manner. Here, the word "diligent" describes those who wisely takes the time to plan out what they're going to do. They investigate, do their homework, and prepare *before* they undertake any new project or venture.

When you arrive at work, are you ready for something specific or will you just dive right in regardless? Do you know what is on your plate for the day or even for the week? Perhaps, like me, you've worked for a boss who would ask something like: "What do you think we ought to work on today?" My initial thought, after exerting a lot of effort to keep my eyes from rolling was "Are you kidding me? If you don't know...we got trouble." Not surprisingly, the company in which that happened went out of business.

It was obvious the boss didn't have a plan. He had no vision for anything new or different. Compare that to another company I worked at where it was common to have the goals for the entire year and the essential outline for reaching them are already laid out and committed to paper by the middle of January. Of course, there were some adjustments made along the way because no matter how well you plan, something always comes up that requires some changes. Typically, those were minimal and reasonably easy to handle. But the vision was there. We knew where we want to go and we had a plan in place on how to get there. That's being diligent.

Imagine any company - from a one-man shop to a corporation with thousands of employees - in which the daily production was based on "what do you think we should do today?" It's not a mystery why organizations that operate in such a manner don't last long. The "reckless only become poor." Even as individuals - if we don't have a plan for tomorrow or next week or next year or our retirement, it is a good bet the future will be a struggle. That's not just me talking. That's the wisdom of the ages...and it's Biblical.

Today, do you have a plan? Have you been diligent in ensuring you know what you're going to do and where it will lead you? No, you won't know every single detail and you will have to adjust here and there but your diligence in setting goals and planning next steps will help you have a clear idea of where your journey will take you. If you don't have that right now - you now have a very important task to do. If you do, good for you! Work the plan. A good plan leads to profit and a good future. Having no plan leads to poverty. Today, be diligent!

"This is the day the Lord has made. Rejoice! And be glad in it." Smile - Step One of a Good Plan: Decide. Do that and all else begins to fall into place. Now get out there and make this a Power Day.

Luke 11: 21: "When a strong man, fully armed, guards his estate, his possessions are secure."

The literal translation says, "his possessions are in peace." Okay, so here we have a strong man who is fully armed. He's guarding his estate. He's taking care of his home, his family, and his stuff. We call that "stewardship" which, in reality, is taking personal responsibility for all with which we've been entrusted.

What is he armed with? God's word. Faith. Love. Wisdom. Good judgment. Common sense. Prayer. The weapons of choice for everyday living and engaging in spiritual battle against an unseen enemy. When a man does this his family, his home and his possessions live in peace. They are secure. Secure from what, exactly? Allowing people, things, and ideas into his home that could infect and negatively affect his wife and children with stuff that does not honor and glorify God. Such things as drugs, the sexually immoral, anger, judgment, lies, hatred, unforgiveness, haughtiness, and more. If he gets careless and lets his guard down; if he fails to take proper actions or lapses into weakness, the risk of losing all his possessions to someone or something grows stronger. The wise and effective course is to get strong and stay strong. God gives us all things. Our part is to be good stewards of what we've been given. If we fail to take proper care, we can lose it. It's a life lesson we teach our kids from an early age that lasts a lifetime. Take care of your stuff. Respect it and remember where it came from. Protect it lest you lose it.

When this Scripture was written, there as many threats as there are today, they were just a bit different back then. Our enemy may not be using spears and arrows or swords, but the devil has any number of ways to introduce trouble to our lives. There are the kids who may not be the best influence on your own children. There are television shows, movies, or songs on the radio that exert a profound influence to steer us away from the path of God. Pick any area of life and you'll find bad influences of every sort. Some are overt and obvious. Others are subtle, even secret.

A strong man, rooted in the Rock of Ages, will be armed, able to resist and guard his family and his possessions. Simple example: You've had a long, tough week. You're tired and really don't feel like going anywhere. It's Sunday morning. Saturday with the kids and that neighborhood thing wore you out more and now it's time to get ready for church. The temptation sounds like this: "God will understand. He'll cut me some slack. I'm tired." Some would think, yeah, well, it's cool. I'll just go to church twice next week or something. A strong man would simply reason - "I could have rested more yesterday and being with my family is a good thing regardless and I will not allow anything, especially a lame excuse, to keep us from doing the most important thing we need to do today." He'd rather take a nap on Sunday afternoon than miss a chance to worship and get spiritually fed and for his kids to do likewise. He is guarding his estate. The one who caves into the excuse will be more easily overtaken. It's the reason Jesus taught us to not give the devil a foothold. Once he has one, he won't stop coming at you.

Today, renew your energy and guard your estate. Be strong. Don't lay down your armor or the weapons God gave you to use. Yes...you can do both - rest and guard - at the same time. Be vigilant always.

"This is the day the Lord has made. Rejoice! And be glad in it." Smile - Knowing your possessions are secure helps you rest better. Now get out there and make this a Power Day.

Ponder This:

"I have never in my life envied a human being who led an easy life; I have envied a great many people who led difficult lives and led them well." **Teddy Roosevelt**

Think about anyone you know personally or know of whose life has always been easy. Theirs is the life that has experienced no major challenges. Their idea of a crisis is not being able to decide what color shirt to wear or "Oh man! We're out of Coco-Puffs!" They've never had to work too hard to get anything and when it comes to going without and having to sacrifice - they truly are clueless or see that as some form of tragedy. Got an idea of that person in mind? Here's the test: Quickly and off the top of your head, think of five personality traits you can honestly say you'd like to emulate about that person and make part of your daily life. Think about it.

May I be a bit more open with you? For me, personally, the life that has been very easy, unmarred by conflict and untested by circumstance strikes me as being unrewarding, unfulfilled, and pretty much a waste of life. Indeed, such a life would be boring.

How might one ever know what their limits are or discover their true strengths and skills and what they are actually capable of without being tested by challenges in their lives? How can one learn to cope with loss or understand the meaning of sacrifice if they've never lost anything they personally worked hard to earn or given up something very dear to them for the sake of someone else or grander purpose? How does one learn be generous; patient or stalwart, what to fear or not fear were it not for the occasional storm of life? A life of ease that is stress free, in my mind, is not the school for such things.

Easy allows for weakness to rule the day in most any situation. *Easy* leads to far more future problems for those who know it as their only experience than for those who understand challenges. A life of ease breeds laziness, selfishness, and the entitlement attitude found in those who believe they deserve something for nothing. It's hard to find anything produced by the *Easy Life* to envy or hold in any esteem whatsoever. Show me the one who is an overcomer. I'll side with those who willingly stand for all they believe in, regardless of cost. My support is for those who won't cave in but persist and keep going anyway. I admire the one who will try when no one else will no matter the outcome. Like you, I respect the one who takes responsibility for his own stuff, his own words, his own deeds and strives to do well. This is the guy who demonstrates a character worth valuing.

Today, there are challenges to be faced, issues to be dealt with, problems to be solved, and questions demanding answers. The extra mile isn't there just for show. It must be traveled. Somebody has to do all that. In **Ezekiel 22:30**, God said He was looking for someone who would stand in the gap but He couldn't find anyone. If God were to take another look, will He see you ready to take that stand? Can you see yourself ready to take that stand? Yeah? Good! Stand up. It's going to be a great day!

"This is the day the Lord has made. Rejoice! And be glad in it." Smile - Learn to handle difficulty well and watch your character grow in great ways. Now get out there and make this a Power Day.

Proverbs 10: 25: "When the storm has swept by, the wicked are gone, but the righteous stand firm forever."

In reading this Proverb, you will want to notice right away that nowhere in these sixteen words does Solomon say or imply that the righteous are exempt from the same storms that hit the unrighteous. He simply said the righteous are rooted in a manner that allows them to stand firm. They weather the storm. They get through it and remain standing. Not so the wicked. The weather doesn't play favorites. Disease doesn't play favorites. Annoying insects couldn't care less who or what anyone is or what their status is – they bite and annoy anyone without discrimination of any sort. Snakes, skunks, wolves, badgers, gators, sharks, thieves, muggers, rain, snow, sleet, and hail….none of those pick and choose whom they will attack. If you're anywhere near where they are, you are a potential target. "Storms" are completely unbiased.

We can define *wicked* people as those who have either forgotten or willfully ignore God and His promises. Consider this: If someone forgets God, upon whom would he rely? Himself or others, maybe. Remember the parable Jesus told of the seeds? Some get tossed onto rock, some fall in with weeds and thorns and some seeds get planted in good soil. The story is similar here. The seed planted in good soil thrives and can weather storms because their roots are firmly anchored to something strong so they can hold on. This allows the plant or tree to stand firm. The seed tossed on hard ground have nothing to root to, there's no anchor. Self is unreliable, biased, and flimsy. Self is not capable of holding a good root. The seed tossed into the weeds got choked out. Others may or may not have good intentions but either way, they can, and will, lead you where you ought not to go.

The righteous - the good seed – takes its root in something bigger and stronger. The righteous seed is anchored to that which is proven reliable, trustworthy, able, and fully capable. Far more so than anything self or others could ever hope to come up with. The righteous have God as their foundation. God! They attach to the Name above all names – the Name to which every knee must bow and thus, the Name that cannot be blown away by a storm but the Name that speaks and calms the storm.

Jesus is the One who commands the storms to be still. Self cannot do that. Others definitely lack that talent. Only God can calm the storm with a word. Storms come along all the time. When a storm blows through your life, take a moment and look around you. See who got blown away and who is still standing firm when the storm ends. It will be easy to see who or what they relied on for help through the storm.

Today, to what are your roots anchored? When - not if, but when - the storms come, stand firm in your faith and on the Rock of Christ Jesus so that when the storm has swept by, you will be found standing firm. Today is a great day to stand up, stand firm, and stand out for Christ.

"This is the day the Lord has made. Rejoice! And be glad in it." Smile - Those rooted in Christ cannot, will not, be "blown away." Now get out there and make this a Power Day.

NOTES

ABOUT THE AUTHOR

Jeffrey Hill graduated from Langston University with a Business Degree with a major in Accounting. He served his country in the military and has invested over 40 years working in the world of business, serving in various leadership positions for companies both in the US and overseas. Jeff found a passion and purpose in writing and transitioned to becoming a Christian author. His first book, *Just A Thought to Make Your Day* was published in 2007. See more at Jeff's blog site: https://know-this.net.

Printed in the United States
by Baker & Taylor Publisher Services